Deepening
Structural Reform in AFRICA
Lessons from EAST ASIA

Editor

LAURA WALLACE

Proceedings of a seminar held in Paris
May 13–14, 1996

International Monetary Fund
Ministry of Finance of Japan

Design and production: IMF Graphics Section

Cataloguing-in-Publication Data

Deepening structural reform in Africa : lessons from East Asia / editor, Laura
Wallace.— Washington, D.C. : International Monetary Fund, [1997]
      p.   cm.
   "Proceedings of a seminar held in Paris, May 13–14, 1996, International
Monetary Fund, Ministry of Finance of Japan."
   ISBN 1-55775-634-1
   1. Structural adjustment (Economic policy) — Africa — Congresses.
2. Africa — Economic policy — Congresses.   I. Wallace, Laura.
II. International Monetary Fund.   III. Japan. ¯Okurash¯o.
   HC800 .D44 1997

Price: $20.00

Address orders to:
International Monetary Fund, Publication Services
700 19th Street, N.W., Washington D.C. 20431, U.S.A.
Telephone: (202) 623-7430
Telefax: (202) 623-7201
E-mail: publications@imf.org
Internet: http://www.imf.org

Preface

THIS VOLUME COVERS the papers and proceedings of the seminar on Deepening Structural Reforms and Policies for Growth in Africa, held in Paris on May 13–14, 1996. The seminar was sponsored by the Japanese Ministry of Finance and jointly organized by the latter and the IMF, in consultation with the World Bank. The seminar was the third of its kind, after the seminar on Policies for Growth in Africa in 1994 (in Tokyo) and on External Assistance and Policies for Growth in Africa in 1995 (in Paris). As in previous seminars, the 1996 seminar brought together senior officials from almost 20 African countries, experts from several Asian and European countries, and senior staff of the IMF, the World Bank, and the OECD.

The seminar's objective was to analyze progress and obstacles for structural reform, derive lessons for Africa from the East Asian experience, and explore ways to accelerate reforms to foster growth in Africa. After years of being battered by terms-of-trade shocks, economic mismanagement, and civil and political turbulence, including recent moves to democracy, many African countries are finally achieving higher growth rates. There is general agreement that macroeconomic stabilization has played a key role in this reversal and that sound and stable macroeconomic policies—budget discipline, relatively low inflation, and realistic exchange rates—as well as open markets are an essential prerequisite for successful reform and sustained growth. However, the question is why the growth response to the improved macroeconomic environment and liberalization of markets has not been stronger and faster. Growth must be much higher to close the gap between Africa and much of the rest of the world within a reasonable time. Most observers agree that the African economies have by and large been successful in implementing the "early stage" of structural reforms, that is, liberalizing exchange systems, opening up trade and payments systems, removing price controls and quantitative restrictions, and liberalizing production and marketing systems, especially in agriculture. But most also agree that the record on the more difficult reforms—involving revenue mobilization, public enterprise restructuring and privatization, and financial sector reform—has been much more uneven. The seminar was therefore cast around the theme of how to accelerate reforms in these three areas, providing policymakers an opportunity to share their hands-on experiences in Africa and Asia and draw lessons for future policies.

In the seminar presentations and discussions, several cross-cutting themes emerged. One was the sequencing and pacing of sectoral reforms, with some participants emphasizing the costs of going too fast, but many others—including most African participants—preferring a faster pace of reform toward market-based monetary, exchange, and financial systems, but with political commitment, coherence, and attention to the supporting institutional and legal changes.

A second theme was the need for a broad political and social acceptance of change and reform; for this, participants agreed, it is essential that policymakers communicate and discuss the costs and benefits of policy options (in particular, the costs of inaction and existing inefficiencies) with all involved, including through a dialogue with the private sector, nongovernmental organizations, and other parts of the civil society. Raising public awareness of the advantages is particularly important for privatization. It is essential to secure both short-term results to sustain the reform process politically as well as long-term results in terms of sustainable reductions in poverty.

A third theme was the need for transparency and accountability in economic management—an important element of good governance—which is seen as socially desirable, favorable to economic growth, and supportive of national ownership of reforms. Good governance is also becoming a more and more important element for donors who, with aid budgets under severe pressure, are seeking an efficient use of their taxpayers' monies through greater selectivity in aid allocation. Finally, continued attention must be paid to how to tailor stabilization and structural measures to individual country circumstances. This implies continuous debate among policymakers, civil society, and external actors on how and how quickly to proceed with reforms and ensure the right institutional environment.

Jack Boorman
Director
Policy Development and Review Department
International Monetary Fund

Acknowledgments

THIS SEMINAR WAS organized by Masato Matsui, Hitoshi Shimura, and Takayuki Yahata of the International Finance Bureau of the Ministry of Finance of Japan; Yoshiyuki Tahara of the Office of the Executive Director for Japan in the International Monetary Fund; and Hiroyuki Hino and Arend Kouwenaar of the International Monetary Fund. Help with the logistical arrangements in Paris was provided by Irène de Heurtaumont of the IMF's Paris Office. I would like to thank Marina Primorac of the IMF's External Relations Department for her skillful style editing and for preparing the volume for publication.

Laura Wallace
Editor

Glossary

CMDT	Compagnie Malienne pour le Développement des Textiles
DAC	Development Assistance Committee
EDI	Economic Development Institute
ESAF	Enhanced Structural Adjustment Facility
IDA	International Development Association
FINSAC	Financial Sector Adjustment Credit
JEXIM	Export–Import Bank of Japan
NERP87	Zambia's New Economic Recovery Program, introduced in 1987
NGO	nongovernmental organization
ODA	Overseas Development Administration
PESAC	Privatization and Enterprise Sector Adjustment Credit
SAF	Structural Adjustment Facility
SPA	Special Programme of Assistance
STF	Systemic Transformation Facility
VAT	value-added tax
WAEMU	West African Economic and Monetary Union

Contents

IV. Future Role of Governments and Donors

The following symbols have been used in this book:

...   to indicate that data are not available;

—   between years or months (e.g., 1995–96 or January–June) to indicate
     the years or months covered, including the beginning and ending years
     or months; and

/   between years (e.g., 1996/7) to indicate a fiscal (financial) year.

"Billion" means a thousand million.

Minor discrepancies between constituent figures and totals are due to
rounding.

The term "country," as used in this volume, does not in all cases refer to a
territorial entity that is a state as understood by international law and practice; the term also covers some territorial entities that are not states, but for
which statistical data are maintained and provided internationally on a separate and independent basis.

Overview

Laura Wallace

A S AFRICA LOOKS for ways to deepen and accelerate the economic reform process, the lessons of the East Asian miracle, of course, come to
mind. That is why on May 13–14, 1996, African and Asian officials and aca-
demics—along with representatives from the IMF, the World Bank, and
other multilateral institutions—met in Paris to exchange experiences. The
hope, as co-chairman Hideichiro Hamanaka of the Ministry of Finance of
Japan put it in his welcoming remarks, was to find hints of innovative approaches to meet the challenges Africa now faces. He cautioned that no single formula would work for every country; rather, the emphasis would have
to be on developing policies tailored for specific countries and regions.
Nonetheless, an exchange of experiences was an excellent starting point, as
each region had valuable lessons to offer.

Session I. Obstacles to Continued Reform

The first session opened with African and Asian perspectives on what
could be done to remove the obstacles to continued reform in Africa.
For Kwesi Botchwey of Ghana, the answer laid in strengthening the design, negotiation, and implementation of adjustment programs, as these
programs provided the overall policy framework for domestic policy reform and external resource transfers. How should this be done? He
cited general agreement on three points.
- Programs should aim at sustainable long-term and broad-based
growth, not just short-term external viability;

1

- Countries should focus more on structural issues (e.g., financial sector reform, public sector reform, and privatization); and
- Countries would benefit from a stable democratic environment that made for transparency and accountability in economic management, and also facilitated popular participation in decision making. As part of this process, governance issues needed to be better articulated, both to determine what fell within the sovereign jurisdiction of the adjusting country and what were the legitimate areas of mutual interest (i.e., between the Bretton Woods institutions and the adjusting country).

On a personal note, he also urged formulating structural targets and conditionality in language and terms that were clear and lent themselves to the least subjective interpretation; improving the adequacy, predictability, and timeliness of external resource flows; and setting up a "Special Program for Clearing the Pipeline of Committed Resources for Africa"—an attempt to at least rationalize those resources already committed to the region.

For Dahlan Sutalaksana of Indonesia, the emphasis was on removing obstacles to economic efficiency and persuading policymakers to hold firm. He noted that since the early 1970s, Indonesia had focused on three key components—getting the prices right, making the market mechanism work, and reducing "bureaucratic costs." Granted, eliminating subsidies sometimes raised questions of political stability, but not acting meant placing a lasting and growing burden on the budget, in turn, draining resources needed for other programs. Similarly, trying to let the market take care of itself would arouse much opposition, but Indonesia's experience suggested that as long as the government held firm, market participants would adjust to the new conditions, although not immediately. Finally, policymakers should not shy from reforming bureaucracies, despite the fact that it took years to succeed. The key here was establishing an environment of discipline and ensuring that the affected bureaucratic elements understood the necessity of reform.

In the general discussion that ensued, it was clear that Botchwey's comments on democracy and governance had hit a nerve, triggering a spirited debate that kept resurfacing throughout the rest of the seminar.[1] Basant Kapur of Singapore set the tone by suggesting that the key question was not whether a democratic or authoritarian regime was needed but rather whether the country was achieving economic growth, a position supported by some of the African participants. What was needed

---

[1] The discussion summaries in the Overview, as well as throughout the volume, highlight key interventions and are not meant to be a summary of all points made.

was market-oriented and outward-oriented strategies that enabled systemic corruption to be reduced and business to be promoted. One might well ask if it was possible to assume that economic growth should come first and democracy second.

Joseph Tsika of Congo noted that his nation, like many others, really had no choice: because of poor economic decisions in the past, they now had to turn to the international community for help, and donors insisted on democracy, even though autocracies had demonstrated the ability to mobilize everyone behind an ideal.

Botchwey responded by defending the need for democracy in Africa: good autocrats were fine so long as they remained good, but when they ceased to be good, there was no way to get rid of them. But should democracy be a condition for financial support? He felt that if the macroeconomic policy framework was sound and the process of resource mobilization and use was transparent and accountable, "the minimum conditions for financial support existed to enable the donors and the adjusting country, through informal dialogue and consultation, to gradually encourage the evolution of a full-fledged democratic environment." He also suggested that the moral strength of the call for democracy by the West was being sapped by a perception in the developing world that when the market was large and the spoils sufficiently attractive, donors found a way of turning their eyes away from obvious abuses, such as in human rights. Finally, Botchwey—supported by other African participants—underscored the importance of dialogue and consultation not just between donors and recipients but also among the various parties in a country.

Session II. How to Accelerate Reform

In the second session, the seminar turned to how reform could be accelerated in the more difficult areas—revenue mobilization, financial sector reform, and public enterprise restructuring and privatization—as opposed to the "early-stage" structural reforms (i.e., liberalizing exchange systems, opening up trade and payments systems, removing price controls and quantitative restrictions, and liberalizing production and marketing systems).

Fiscal and Financial Sector Reforms

Peter Heller of the IMF started out by noting that an adequate non-inflationary revenue mobilization effort was critical for financing a government's necessary social and economic expenditure obligations. Yet, in sub-Saharan Africa, the tax effort in two-thirds of the countries had been disappointingly low, with tax revenue at or below 15 percent of GDP; indeed, almost one-third had ratios below 10 percent of GDP. How could African governments boost these ratios? He suggested that they focus on strengthening both tax policy and tax and customs administration, as was being successfully done in Benin, Burkina Faso, Gabon, and Uganda. Key measures should include reducing and controlling exemptions, simplifying tax structures, reducing reliance on trade taxes, introducing a simplified form of the value-added tax, simplifying the approach to taxing small enterprises, and relying on an integrated rather than a piecemeal approach to tax policy.

Shahid Yusuf of the World Bank, in commenting on the paper, agreed with Heller's assessment of the challenges facing African countries in mobilizing tax revenues. But on the question of tax/GDP ratios, he noted that the picture was less grim if the sample was enlarged from 29 to include the remaining 13 sub-Saharan countries—as seven of these had ratios greater than 15 percent and only three were 10 percent or below. Moreover, on average, tax/GDP ratios in Africa were comparable to those of East Asian countries in the 1970s, and East Asia only began introducing significant reforms in the early to mid-1980s. What was most striking about East Asia's fiscal experience was that expenditure management, rather than an extraordinary tax effort, was the principal achievement, and it contributed to the increase in national savings that substantially explained East Asia's growth performance.

The question of sequencing and pacing of reforms—another theme throughout the seminar—first surfaced in a presentation on financial reform by David Cole (and Betty Slade), formerly of the Harvard Institute for International Development. Given the many serious disruptions and financial crises associated with recent attempts to modernize, privatize, and increase the market orientation of financial systems in African countries, he said, policymakers might want to consider a more gradual, market-building approach, one that operated on a time frame of one or two decades rather than a few years. Countries should not try to push their system ahead too rapidly, because a misstep could slow down the entire liberalization process.

Tetsuji Tanaka of Japan suggested that a key influence in both the possibility of a shift toward a market economy and the pace of reform would be historical and cultural conditions. He noted that some say "ethics and a philosophy that includes asceticism are required to operate a capitalist market economy." As evidence, they point to the roles of the Protestant ethic of nineteenth century Europe and Confucianism in East Asia (i.e., helping to nurture the necessary stoicism and desire to abide by contracts). He felt that market participants must be "ascetic" (laying aside their own interests) and "fair" from a social point of view, and technocrats should be trained to perform with a high degree of integrity. As for what lessons East Asia could offer not only Africa but also Central Asian economies, such as the Kyrgyz Republic, that were attempting a takeoff with scarce accumulated capital, Tanaka underscored the importance of channeling public funds to the market and letting the government set priorities for distributing the funds. The degree of market intervention should be dictated by the development stage of each economy; the number of market participants; the degree of market maturity; the market practices; and history, culture, and religion.

In the comments that followed, both Kapur of Singapore and Patrick Downes of the IMF raised questions about the workability of a number of the suggestions in the Cole and Slade paper on a more gradual approach to financial sector reform, particularly in the areas of monetary policy management and prudential management of banks.

As for the pace of reform, Downes agreed with Cole that sometimes financial reforms failed, at least temporarily, because the authorities attempted to go too fast or because some of the concomitant reforms were not present, such as fiscal consolidation and effective banking supervision capability. But he cautioned that in an era of economic globalization and integrated financial markets—and particularly the availability of vastly enlarged amounts of private international capital—one must ask whether the relative costs and benefits for Africa of opening up its financial markets only slowly were the same as those faced in Asia when these countries had made their decisions regarding liberalization. He argued that "there is a danger that countries in Africa, the poorer countries, may be marginalized and left behind—all the more so as official aid flows start to dry up and the large private capital flows increasingly gravitate to emerging market countries." Moreover, delaying financial reforms often worsened existing problems in the monetary and banking system.

Turning to Tanaka's paper, Downes agreed with the importance of an appropriate work and business ethic, but questioned Tanaka's call for more state intervention. Rather, a more activist stance was required in championing the cause of free markets in countries like the Kyrgyz Republic, even more so perhaps than in Africa where the historical experience had been quite different. He noted that financial reform was a continuous process, and thus it would be a waste of resources to develop market institutions and implement financial reforms without adhering to them.

Tanaka's suggestions on government intervention (and the Cole and Slade call for a more gradual approach to financial sector reform), however, found support from Tadahiko Nakagawa of the Export-Import Bank of Japan. He drew on Japan's recent experiences in countries such as Tunisia and Hungary to argue that "although a market approach serves as a sound basis for financial reform, some types of creative interventions and controls—in this case, our two-step loans—can help support or complement the market system," paving the way for future financial reform in countries at a transitional stage of development. Although Japan had yet to try such two-step loans in Africa—whereby Japan lends money to a bank (or banks) in a particular country, and the bank then onlends the money to individual enterprises—it was contemplating doing so.

In the discussion that ensued, most participants focused on the pacing and sequencing of reforms. In the fiscal area, the African representatives suggested that the problem was one of timing, not one of whether the IMF's suggested reforms should be adopted. If countries reduced export taxes too rapidly, trying to replace them with domestic consumption taxes, difficulties arose because most African economies were rural and agricultural in nature, and the informal sector was still large. In addition, it was often hard to reduce and eliminate tax exemptions, as most were linked to investment codes and most developing countries offered such exemptions. Further, they noted that donors could help by ensuring that funds arrived on time.

In the financial area, although some participants favored a more gradual approach, the general consensus among the Africans present was that they could not afford to proceed at the pace that some Asian economies had adopted, given the changed economic environment. As Soumaïla Cissé of Mali put it, Africa had to accelerate or risk being swept out of the way. Moreover, several speakers pointed to cases where quick moves to market-oriented systems had helped to depersonalize and depoliticize decision making.

Parastatal Reform and Privatization

On the privatization front, John Nellis of the World Bank noted that there had been a decline worldwide in the number, as well as in the economic and financial weight, of state-owned enterprises over the past decade. But in Africa, parastatals still accounted for a large amount of economic activity (as measured by GDP), nonagricultural employment, and investment—despite the recent spurt of privatizations. This situation is a problem because these entities consume about 20 percent of available human and physical capital in the region, while contributing only about 10 percent of value added. What are the key obstacles? Nellis pointed to lingering government fears that unemployment would rise, that the only buyers would be seen as undesirable (e.g., foreigners, a particular ethnic group, or well-connected domestic elites), that sources of patronage and perquisites would be lost, or that deindustrialization would result. He urged African governments to move quickly on privatizing those parastatals producing tradable products and operating in competitive, or potentially competitive markets, and to involve the private sector in running the infrastructure parastatals.

But Yasuo Yokoyama of Mitsui and Co. saw the time frame rather differently. "Rapid privatization will not produce the desired good results," he maintained, "but instead only pose further difficulties for the business sector." Countries should take a leaf out of Japan's book and spend the next 50–100 years establishing sound economic fundamentals before embarking on privatizations.

Two African speakers—Jean-Claude Brou of Côte d'Ivoire and Cissé of Mali—however, saw no reason to defer privatization, underscoring all the progress that had been made in their countries in recent years. Brou said that ideally five conditions should be in place: a balanced macroeconomic environment; a competitive market; full political support as well as the support of a majority of the people; the prior definition of a clear, transparent, and rigorous process; and a flexible, pragmatic approach to implementation. But if there were sectors where a competitive market was not yet a reality, certain interim measures could be taken. For example, in the electricity sector in his country, the government and the private operator of the electricity network had signed an agreement defining their respective responsibilities, especially on establishing rates.

In the discussion that followed, most African participants cited their own instances of progress on the privatization front, stressing that the remaining obstacles were largely political and social, not just technical. Several speakers pointed to the challenge of convincing unions, parliaments, and political parties to embrace privatization when the costs were immediate, while the benefits were long term and diffuse. Mary Muduuli of Uganda noted that her country was only now waking up to the need to put advertisements in the media to explain the advantages of privatization.

But the African participants also felt that the multilateral institutions and donors could help by not setting structural targets and conditions that were unrealistic and even perverse—a case in point being the "fire sales" that can result when a set number of firms in a targeted sector must be privatized by a certain date. And they took strong issue with Yokoyama's suggestion, which they viewed as provocative, that Africa would need to wait decades before it could successfully tackle privatizations.

Session III. Enhancing the Effectiveness of External Assistance

In the third session, the debate turned to experiences with structural adjustment programs that had been supported by the IMF and World Bank, both from the point of view of recipients and donors.

Zéphirin Diabré of Burkino Faso led off his paper by suggesting that since these programs were the target of fairly harsh criticism, it was important to determine how they could be improved.[2] His recommendations include ensuring that the strategic view of development is internalized (i.e., national leaders prepare the draft programs); poverty reduction is the primary objective; the social dimension is recognized and conditionality reduced; the general public understands the programs; and adjustment has a regional dimension. He called for another approach to conditionality, involving greater recognition of individual country capabilities and constraints and greater promptness in disbursements. He also observed that "the general impression is that the emphasis is on restoring macroeconomic equilibria at the expense of bona fide development."

As for Zambia, Jacob Mwanza said that his country's experiences with adjustment programs since the early 1970s showed that stabilization measures were easier to implement than structural adjustment measures, as the latter required striking and maintaining a careful balance between tight and expansionary monetary and fiscal policies. He emphasized the importance of appropriate economic policies, but noted that, in the end, they could do little more than permit, or at most, encourage a better economic performance—also critical was establishing an institutional framework to support the "correct" policies. Zambia's prospects for economic recovery and sustainable development now depended critically on sound economic management and external support. But at the same time, debilitating external debt loads had to be resolved.

On the donor side, Michael Foster of the Overseas Development Administration (ODA) in the United Kingdom explored the recent switch from the traditional project approach to a sector-wide approach, now a central element of the World Bank's lending strategy in Africa. He said the context for the switch was twofold: weaknesses in African budgets and budget management (e.g., large deficits that strangle private access to credit, poor levels of accountability, and poorly targeted subsidies and spending priorities); and the fact that donors themselves had contributed

---

[2]Zéphirin Diabré was unable to attend the seminar but submitted a paper.

significantly to the budget problems (e.g., by giving too much project aid relative to resources for operation and maintenance, undermining local management capacity, and often escaping budget disciplines).

Foster said the sector-wide approach, which was part of the evolving consensus on new conditionality, hinged on a medium-term expenditure framework that determined the size of the resource envelope for the sector, and the government drawing up a comprehensive program for the sector that was agreed with the donors. Key factors for success included: strong leadership from the government side, macroeconomic stability and predictable budgets, adequate commitment and motivation of those required to change their behavior, confidence in the accounting arrangements, donors' willingness to merge their efforts and accept lower visibility of their own funds, and donors not forcing the pace on governments or other donors.

In commenting on the papers, Peter Warutere of Kenya remarked that the recent growth pickup in sub-Saharan Africa as a whole seemed to stem in part from strong structural reforms. Until recently, he noted, many African leaders viewed such reforms with suspicion, given that many donors were also demanding political democratization, and the programs were being prescribed by outsiders unfamiliar with the intricate domestic conditions. But in recent years, donors had recognized the need to mobilize popular support for reforms. Indeed, Kenya's decision to publicly debate its 1996–98 Policy Framework Paper—which was designed by the government, with assistance from the IMF and World Bank staffs—was part of this process.

From the Asian side, Masako Ii of Japan struck an upbeat note by suggesting that recent studies on the impact of adjustment programs on social sectors did not show a major cut in the expenditure share of health and education, although they did show some expenditure misallocation within a given social sector (for example, expenditures should be targeted at priority programs that benefited the poor most, such as primary education or basic health, rather than at salary supplements). Moreover, she felt that simple measurement errors might be responsible for the pessimism about saving, investment, employment, and growth in Africa, as official statistics (both of the international financial institutions and African governments) underestimated economic activity by excluding data from the informal sector.

In the following discussion, the main concern was how to get the desired supply response in African nations, particularly in the productive, as opposed to the social, sectors. Cole asked if the kind of infrastructure and other elements that would support such a rapid supply response were much less readily available in Africa than they had been in South Korea in the mid-1960s and Indonesia in the late 1960s.

On the topic of ownership and conditionality, several Africans expressed frustration with donor conditionality and lack of transparency, and what they perceived to be shifting goalposts whenever they were about to score a goal. Warutere raised questions about donor consistency on such sensitive issues as human rights and pointed to instances of inflexible conditionality in privatization. What should be done if buyers could not be found for enterprises, even after they had been advertised several times? How could the government avoid charges of corruption if the enterprises in the end were sold to the highest bidders, but the bids were less than half the valuation price?

Session IV. Future Role of Governments and Donors

Mark Baird of the World Bank opened the panel discussion by noting that what was striking at the seminar was the broad acceptance of the need to undergo adjustment. There were clear concerns, however, about the need to secure both short-term results to sustain the reform process politically and long-term results that delivered on promised reductions in poverty—prompting him to urge countries to persevere with adjustment. "All the evidence clearly shows that when you implement sound macroeconomic policies, you do get a supply response." But in Africa progress in policy reform had been uneven, with slippages, raising questions about the credibility of the programs.

World Bank colleague Ravi Kanbur observed that over the past few years, the dialogue between Asia and Africa had been maturing and deepening, with the realization that there was not *the* East Asian miracle, but rather many East Asian miracles, each with its own peculiarities; and, of course, there was not a single Africa, but many Africas. Thus, country specificity should be the basis of the future dialogue.

Kanbur highlighted three issues that merited more discussion: culture, timing, and conditionality. On *culture,* everyone accepted that it was important for economic growth, but the connection needed to be explored. For example, Tetsuji Tanaka had mentioned that many observers point to the vital role of Confucianism in East Asia in terms of instilling the proper ethics and philosophy required to operate a capitalist market economy—yet only 40–50 years ago, many observers had cited Confucianism for the slow economic progress in East Asia.

On *timing,* it was doubtful that Africa really had 50 years to get its economic fundamentals right before proceeding with privatization. So how could Africa get its desired "quick growth," in light of points raised by Cole and others that moving too quickly could sometimes backfire? And on *conditionality,* as countries moved more deeply into structural reform, the number of paradoxes that arose underscored the need for re-thinking the links between conditionality, ownership, and policy reform. For example, Western commentators often cited land reform in East Asia as a key policy reform, yet land reform was imposed by an occupying military power. And some countries proposed reform programs, presumably demonstrating ownership, that donors refused to accept. Perhaps part of the answer lay in the technical solutions suggested by Baird, such as disconnecting the resource flow from the satisfaction of specific conditionalities in tricky areas (e.g., civil service reform and privatization).

Speaking for the OECD, Richard Carey stressed the new emphasis on "development partnerships"—a term that derived from four major changes. First, donors and recipients had moved from viewing conditionality as a cost of access to external resources to thinking in terms of policy reform as the path to sustainable development. The question was no longer whether to engage in policy reform, but how to do it, and Africans themselves were fully engaged in the process. Second, there had been a shift from short-term to long-term adjustment perspectives, with a concern for sustainability (economic, social, environmental, cultural, and political). As part of this, there was also a recognition of the key role of institutional and capacity development. Third, the "results culture" put the spotlight on what everyone's efforts added up to, underscoring the need for coordination and integrated sector approaches. Fourth, a shift in accountability philosophies meant focusing more on what was being done with balance of payments and budget support in terms of resource allocation, particularly through the public budget. As a result of these changes, Carey said the OECD was undertaking a number of new initiatives, including in the area of governance.

On governance, Hiroyuki Hino of the IMF noted that there was a growing consensus that economic governance issues—such as lack of transparency in budgetary procedures and corruption—played an important role in investment and savings decisions and ultimately economic growth. Rebutting suggestions that perhaps economic governance was not that critical, given that some countries had grown rapidly despite widespread corruption, he said such arguments overlooked the concern that the efficiency of resource allocation was undermined by corruption. Possible remedies might include closing avenues for rent seeking; setting up a system that would assure full transparency in public finance; strictly enforcing a civil service code of conduct; and establishing a civil service that was lean, efficient, and properly remunerated.

But when it came to noneconomic governance issues, such as democratization, Hino said the link with economic performance was more complex. He pointed to the range of opinions expressed at the seminar, with some speakers confident that good political governance was essential for good economic performance, and others wondering whether democracy of the Westminster type was necessary for economic development in all African countries. Nonetheless, it was important to recognize that most bilateral donors saw a vital link between open, democratic, and accountable systems of governance and respect for human rights on the one hand, and the ability to achieve sustained economic and social development on the other. Indeed, a number of these donors, facing ever tighter budgetary constraints, were linking their assistance to the political aspects of good governance. With Africa still heavily dependent on donor help, that reality meant that Africa would have to develop a constructive approach to deal with donors on a broad range of governance issues.

Tour de Table

In the final tour de table, several key themes emerged.

Culture. Mwanza observed that the seminar had opened a window of opportunity for his country and the African continent to explore economic models of development that stood as alternatives to traditional Western ones. The key ingredient for success, across cultures, looked to be the consistent pursuit and implementation of sound macroeconomic policies. However, Toshio Fujinuma of Japan cautioned that taking culture into account did not mean just picking the best model for rapid economic growth but, rather, instigating changes in social values or behavior patterns.

Lessons from East Asia. Kapur emphasized the importance of an outward-oriented trade and investment strategy to boost economic efficiency and competitiveness. Such a strategy involved getting prices right, pursuing wide-ranging economic and social infrastructure improvements, attracting direct foreign investment, and insisting on good governance. Tanaka added that the exact recipe would vary from country to country, reflecting diverse starting points and differences among countries, such as in culture.

Governance. Several speakers picked up on Hino's distinction between economic and noneconomic governance, with general agreement that good governance, however defined, was vital for economic growth. Joseph Kinyua of Kenya stressed that a lack of good economic governance gave rise to wasted resources and investment distortions, making it harder to raise living standards. Moreover, it was difficult to achieve good economic governance without also securing good noneconomic governance, which formed the basis for political stability. But Luc Oy-oubi of Gabon wondered whether everyone in the seminar meant the same thing when talking about democracy, as some seemed to feel that there were only good elements. Certainly, freedom of enterprise was favorable, but output lost to strikes was not.

Conditionality. On the need to rethink conditionality, Foster of ODA noted that the key problem he observed with conditionality was that it prevented credibility. It was private investors, not donors, who needed to be convinced. Thus, recipient governments should take ownership of their programs and convince investors that they would remain committed. Cole urged donors and recipients to operate as allies, not adversaries. As evidence, he cited the cases of Korea in the mid-1960s and Indonesia in the late 1960s, both of which enjoyed turning points when there was a close alliance between donors and recipients.

Timing. African participants once again expressed their eagerness to move forward as quickly as possible, with Brou stressing that Africa could not afford the luxury to wait decades to replicate the East Asian miracle. But Cole maintained his voice of caution on financial sector reform, and several Asian speakers reiterated their preference for a more gradual approach. Nakagawa noted that "even if an issue is burning, we must think first." Nonetheless, he underscored the international community's responsibility to help Africa in its time of need, looking for optimism in the fact that many Africans at the seminar had cited growing signs of private sector development.

Concluding Remarks

In the concluding remarks, co-chairman Jack Boorman of the IMF observed that one unmistakable message of the seminar was that the politics of structural reform were tough. Participants agreed that more effort should go into communicating costs and benefits of policy options so that policymakers could enlist the support of their own civil societies—especially the private sector—for reform.

But as the dialogue accelerated, pressures for democratization and good governance would only grow. Boorman cited the widespread acceptance of the view that good governance—defined to include greater transparency and accountability in the conduct of governments—was socially desirable, that it could have a positive effect on growth, and that it was increasingly and inevitably a concern of donors. At the same time, new ways had to be found to craft programs and sector projects in a way that assured donors that their monies were being well spent while permitting governments to retain "ownership" of their reforms. He noted that many participants felt that good governance and democracy were the same thing and "there needs to be more exploration county by country, and perhaps with more subtlety, in the search for democratic processes appropriate to the conditions of Africa."

Can Africa simply copy what worked best in East Asia and hope for a similar takeoff in the years to come? Boorman said that participants felt that the economic environment had changed dramatically since the East Asian countries established the basis for their spectacular growth. "The message that came through this discussion seemed to be that the cost of acting slowly—and forgoing the benefits that faster access to outside capital and technology can provide—is too dear."

SESSION I

Progress and Challenges in Structural Reform

1

Opening Remarks

Hideichiro Hamanaka

WELCOME TO the Third African-Asian joint meeting on Policies for Growth in Africa, organized by the Government of Japan, the International Monetary Fund, and the World Bank. We are delighted to see many of you again and to welcome new participants from Africa, Asia, North America, and Europe.

Let me begin by trying to bring you up to date on our mission. At the Halifax Summit, the Group of Seven Ministers urged the Development Committee to establish a task force to debate the roles of multilateral development banks, such as the World Bank, the African Development Bank, and the Asian Development Bank. The task force met seven times—I attended five of these meetings—and in the end, we produced a report entitled *Serving a Changing World,* which was welcomed and endorsed by the Development Committee this past April. A number of points emerged when we finally concluded our report, including the following:

- There is a need for good governance.
- There is a need for more local responsibility, taking into account the institutional capabilities and the absorptive capacity of borrowing countries.
- There is a need for a result-oriented culture, replacing the approval culture that has predominated for so long. Although it is clear that this point was made with respect to multilateral banks, I believe that development will surely come when recipient countries take result-oriented approaches.
- There is a need for paying due attention to the diverse situation of countries, in terms of poverty, culture, history, and different develop-

17

ment experiences—in other words, there is a need for country- and re-
gion-specific policies.
  • There is a need for encouraging investment flows and development
of the private sector.
  These conclusions could be compared with those of the World Bank's
1993 report, *The East Asian Miracle*.[1] This report was a milestone in economic theory and development policy, as it was the first to analyze the
successful economic growth of East Asian countries. The report told us:
  • domestic savings are critical for development;
  • human resources, among others, are important when, or even be-
    fore, development really takes place;
  • good governance and responsible administrators are necessary; and
  • it is vital to have a medium- and long-term growth strategy—or,
    in other words, consistency over time.
  Yes, the world has changed. These two reports look alike and yet,
upon closer observation, look different.
  Let me turn now to Africa. During the 1980s, Africa suffered from a
continual worsening in economic conditions, aggravated by a serious
drought. We noticed real GNP fell; interest rates rose; and debt accumulated—with the ratio of debt to GNP skyrocketing from about
20 percent in 1980 to 80 percent in 1987.
  But since then, progress has been made in many areas. Many countries have introduced the multiparty system, adopted democratic con-
stitutions, and are now enjoying free and open elections. Economic reforms are being initiated and strengthened. Privatization of state-owned
enterprises has started. Rigid regulations have been relaxed, and among
other things, exchange rate policy has changed. Moreover, the IMF's
most recent *World Economic Outlook* says that growth performance in
Africa is expected to continue to improve on the basis of the stronger
macroeconomic and structural policies implemented by many countries
in recent years.
  Even so, although a number of countries are performing well—and
some governments are really trying to strive for growth—there are a
number that still remain in poverty, meaning we still have a long way to
go.
  Now, I need to comment on Asia. For over 30 years, Asia and the
Pacific Rim have enjoyed a high rate of growth. Needless to say,
Asians worked hard, from dawn to dusk. They worked for their large
families, for their communities, and for their countries. Investment

[1]World Bank, *The East Asian Miracle: Economic Growth and Public Policy* (Washington: World
Bank, 1993).

rates remained high; savings rates were higher; and financial structures reorganized. Today, Asia absorbs a huge amount of foreign direct investment. However, I have to tell you that everything is not fine in Asia.

In the Asia Pacific region, there are still 700 million people living on less than $1 a day. We observe rural poverty, especially in provinces remote from booming cities. For example, poverty exists in the southern India plateau, the Ganges River basin, the central and northwestern provinces of China, and the Pacific island economies. In addition, we note urban poverty. There are huge cities, megacities, in Asia, probably with populations of over ten million. These megacities have many poor people, sometimes living in slums, with no water supply, no electricity supply, and no sewers. As these countries grow, people will migrate from rural areas to cities. Urban development is a challenge, too.

What can be done to help lift the world's poor out of poverty? One way, as you all know, is through the World Bank's International Development Association (IDA). In late 1994, I joined the IDA-11 replenishment talks in Madrid as a chief negotiator representing the Government of Japan. The path from Madrid to the final meeting in Tokyo, which was this past March, took 18 months. In ordinary cases, five or six meetings would have been sufficient, but this time we needed nine or ten. The challenge was balancing the need for concessional funds with the reality of the fiscal difficulties that advanced countries face.

IDA will soon be reported on to the Governors, and the Governors will be asked to agree to the eleventh replenishment in the coming months. Roughly half of the IDA money will be utilized to establish infrastructures, educational facilities, and electricity supplies in Africa. I would like to mention that as Japan became the largest donor to IDA-11, it kept its 20 percent share of the replenishment, followed by the United States at about 13 or 14 percent, then France, Germany, and other European colleagues.

For our seminar here in Paris, we have brought distinguished speakers from Africa, Asia, Europe, and North America. During the first day, we will explore the progress and challenges of structural reform in Session I, how to accelerate reform in Session II, and how to enhance the effectiveness of external assistance in Session III. For the second day, we will have a panel discussion on the future role of governments and donors, during which I hope we will have a heated debate, with ample time for interventions and rebuttals. Out of the debate, I think we will probably find hints of innovative approaches to meet the challenges Africa now faces.

Distinguished guests, no single formula will work for all countries. Rather, we need to develop policies tailored for specific countries and regions. Nonetheless, we will try to focus on the experiences of countries in other parts of the world, as they have valuable lessons to offer.

We have a good climate to develop South-to-South cooperation, which is a new challenge. We need more Asians with development success to work in Africa. I believe and hope that by the end of the two days, Asian and African participants will have benefited from attending this meeting as friends, as the world is so small and our economies are so interdependent.

2

Obstacles to Continued Reform: An African Perspective

Kwesi Botchwey

IN RECENT YEARS, growth rates in sub-Saharan African countries have improved somewhat on the average, but they are still suboptimal and sluggish in spite of many years of economic adjustment. At the same time, the region's marginalization continues even in international trade, which, given our increasingly globalized world economy, offers perhaps the most credible path to faster growth. Against this background, adjustment programs provide an overall policy framework for domestic policy reform and external resource transfers. But they must be strengthened in their design, negotiation, and implementation, if the fundamental goals of economic development are to be realized.

The debate on ways of improving these programs has begun in earnest within the World Bank and the IMF and also within the African/donor circles, where there is renewed interest in the matter. Indeed, a number of very useful proposals are already on the table. But even as the debate progresses, adjustment programs continue to be designed and implemented without much change. It is thus important that the debate be better focused and punctuated, so that points of general agreement can be made to inform the continuing adjustment experience. I propose to highlight what I see as major areas of convergence that are emerging in the debate and also to offer some reflections of my own, drawing on Ghana's experience.

Broad Areas of Consensus

Leaving aside some rather interesting theoretical and "political" issues that are raised in assessments of the results of adjustment programs in Africa, there is general agreement that Africa has seen major improvements in the macroeconomic and trade areas, but less spectacular gains in the real sector (especially in agriculture), the financial sector, and public enterprise reform. There is also general agreement on a number of ways of improving programs.

First, these programs should aim at sustainable long-term and broad-based growth, as opposed to just short-term external viability. This must mean more than the mere adoption of the Policy Framework Paper (PFP) mechanism for country programs. There are both political and economic aspects to the matter. The way forward is for the external agents of reform to provide support for the government's own long-term policy framework, designed to stimulate accelerated and sustained growth. Such a long-term policy framework requires for its credibility and sustainability a broad national consensus and the government's *leadership* and *commitment*. Government leadership of the process is absolutely vital, and if it is perceived that a government does not have the capacity to develop its own medium- to long-term vision, it must be encouraged or prodded in the informal consultations that precede formal negotiations to "acquire" this capacity; there is abundant African and other expertise on the market. Such a national program in which the objectives, costs, and trade-offs are defined and, where possible, quantified is crucial for national debate and consensus building. The ownership does not lie in the nationality of the authoring of the program as such, although in the normal course of things, the participation by agents of the government in the program's preparation would be logical. Rather, it lies in the conscious and deliberate choice by the government of the reform path as a way of realizing its long-term objectives—and not as a painful or, worse still, a little-understood expedient for gaining access to international assistance and acceptability.

Second, adjustment programs need to focus more on the structural issues—specifically, to quicken the pace of reform in the financial sector, the private sector environment, and the state-owned enterprise system.

Third, countries would benefit from a stable democratic environment that makes for transparency and accountability in economic management generally, and also facilitates popular participation in decision-making, especially at the grassroots level. There is one other issue to be addressed here.

Governance issues have come to be expressed in ways that do not sufficiently acknowledge their universal character—corruption is certainly not a peculiarly African disease! As a result, the governance debate has tended to focus on sanctions for corruption and malfeasance. The concern, however, should be to liberalize the macroeconomic as well as the legal and administrative apparatus, so as to curtail the incentive and space for rent seeking, and to subject the mobilization and use of public resources and the entire regime of public works and service contracts to the general oversight of democratic institutions—parliamentary finance committees, public accounts committees, Account-Generals' Offices, and Auditor-Generals' Offices, endowed with the competence and constitutional mandate to protect the integrity of public expenditure. The idea is not to chase thieves on some *ad hoc* basis at the behest of donors, but to create democratic institutions that can operate their own surveillance mechanisms and deal with cases of malfeasance in clear and predictable ways. The governance issues, moreover, need to be better articulated, to determine both what lies within the sovereign jurisdiction of the adjusting country, and what are the legitimate areas of mutual interest, as between the Bretton Woods institutions and the adjusting country.

Some Personal Thoughts

To these broad areas of consensus, I should like to add the following.

First, with the renewed and, I might add, welcome interest in the structural issues, there is an urgent need to formulate structural targets and conditionality in language and terms that are clear and lend themselves to the least subjective interpretation. In the past, there has been a tendency to use vague and sometimes even self-defeating terms (such as when prospective buyers of state-owned enterprises *know* in advance that the country *must* sell a given number of enterprises by a given date). Additionally, the public sector reform agenda, including civil service and state enterprise reform, must be driven by country-specific market and efficiency considerations—as opposed to a predisposition to particular forms of ownership and generalized norms for downsizing. Equally important, the short- (and longer-) run financial costs of such reform must be explicitly acknowledged in the macroeconomic and financial program that the country commits itself to implement.

Second, countries need to be able to rely on the *adequate, predictable,* and *timely* external resource flows from both bilateral and multilateral sources. The shock that can be caused by shortfalls in external flows meant for budgetary or balance of payments support can be every bit as destabilizing as a severe drought or massive terms-of-trade loss. Ghana's experience, especially since 1992, amply demonstrates this. In 1992 these shortfalls amounted to 1.8 percent of GDP; in 1993, 1.6 percent; in 1994, as much as 3.6 percent; and in 1995, 1 percent. What is worse, the fiscal shocks caused by these shortfalls can severely disrupt the fiscal situation for several years (especially when they are financed through bank borrowing), because of their impact on the stock of domestic debt as well as the cost of servicing it.

Third, there is an urgent need to resolve what I call the "tail-chasing" syndrome in policy-based lending: external flows are withheld because some structural conditionality has been breached; the withholding of funds leads to a deterioration in the fiscal and, therefore, the overall macroeconomic situation; and this in turn leads to a further withholding of committed program loans and grants since the stability of the macroeconomic environment is a general condition for disbursement of such loans and grants.

Fourth, while Bank/Fund coordination has improved tremendously in recent years, a great deal more needs to be done to improve coordination within the Bank, especially between "policy" and "sector" departments. Furthermore, as every practitioner knows, the agenda for the reform and improvement of donor coordination is still unfinished. A great deal more needs to be done to achieve improved policy cohesion and relieve pressure on local administrative capacity.

Finally, I would like to make a proposal, at this stage provisionally in the hope that if the idea is at least acceptable in principle, the ball can be caught in flight and worked over by a special task force to bring it closer to negotiation and implementation. (1) Net aid flows to the African region are now said to be positive and favorable compared to flows to other regions. But even then, the situation is not quite so favorable when the flows are netted off against terms-of-trade losses. (2) By all accounts, and by every prognosis, the prospects of a real increase in aid over the medium to long term are not good. (3) The flow of foreign direct investment to sub-Saharan Africa is still a trickle compared to other regions. While the situation is reversible, experience suggests that this is going to take time, and depends in part on the perceptions of investors and the advantages of size and geography—not just on the will and commitment of the African countries. (4) In order, therefore, not to throttle the African development effort or condemn it to slow growth—growth constrained by the "realities" of external resource flows and the "most realistic" assumptions on the prospects of further growth of domestic revenues (5 percent of real GDP growth is fast becoming the limit of "realism")—I call for a Special Program for Clearing the Pipeline of Committed Resources for Africa. I have in mind here more than the Bank's usual portfolio reviews.

My point is that at a time of resource stringency in Africa, and in order to accelerate growth rates in the region, there is a lot to be said for freeing resources *already* committed, for use in funding new priority investments carefully negotiated between the partners. The idea calls for some innovation and creativity in channeling these resources. Accordingly, the well-known bureaucratic and administrative shackles that bedevil the use of these resources must be avoided. New areas of priority investment in infrastructure, human resource development, and export promotion and diversification—especially for low value-added manufacturers—can be boosted this way over the next five years, thereby improving the supply response to adjustment measures. The program thus calls for a consolidation and quick reprogramming of pipeline resources that by all accounts are large and whose slow disbursement is often cited as evidence of Africa's weak absorptive capacity. Side by side with the freeing of already committed resources, the issues of trade access and private investment promotion must be central to the new orientation of the Bank, especially in the coming years.

I realize, of course, that this proposal will need to be worked through to make it implementable. Not all committed resources are in disbursement arrears, and there are rules about moving resources from projects to program applications. But my point is that, given the critical and yet potentially hopeful situation that Africa faces today, a great deal can be achieved by rationalizing resources already committed to the region.

3

Obstacles to Continued Reform: Indonesia's Experience

Dahlan M. Sutalaksana

WHEN INDONESIA EMBARKED on a more rational attempt to develop its economy at the end of the 1960s, it designed a series of economic reforms to support the implementation of its string of Five Year Plans. I would like to briefly review these reforms and the motivations behind them, and then see what lessons we can draw from Indonesia's experience in overcoming obstacles to continued reform.

Economic Reforms in the 1970s

The first major reform was the liberalization of the foreign exchange system in 1971, replacing the previously controlled regime. The objective was to restore the balance of payments to a sustainable position, as it had severely deteriorated since the early 1960s because of the previous government's inappropriate policies. Given that Indonesia is a long stretch of islands, with a heavy dependence on international trade, a liberal foreign exchange system was considered to be a precondition for building a strong international base for the economy.

Nevertheless, this policy was not without difficulties. Following the collapse of the Bretton Woods system in the early 1970s, which gave rise to more active—and, at times, volatile—international capital movements, there was a need for a more flexible domestic monetary policy to minimize the impact of this volatility on the economy. One of the necessary conditions for a successful liberal foreign exchange policy is to avoid excessive domestic inflation, while keeping interest rates at competitive levels. In principle, the rule is to create a stable economic environment by sticking to a balanced budget policy, sterilizing capital inflows, and attuning bank credit expansion to the required level of money demand.

Soon after Indonesia began implementing its first Five Year Plan, it became clear that oil would serve as the major determinant of economic growth. Indeed, the record shows that during 1973–83, the economy was extremely dependent upon oil exports. Oil exports were the main source of foreign exchange reserves. Government revenues from oil averaged 52 percent of total government revenues annually and 64 percent of total domestic revenues.

The oil windfall led to a large increase in liquidity and brought renewed inflationary pressures. Thus, in an effort to avoid the negative effects of the oil boom on economic stabilization—and economic development in general—the government adopted a monetary policy based on the use of direct controls. In April 1974, the government imposed credit ceilings on individual banks, along with interest rate ceilings on state bank loans and deposits, as a means of checking excessive domestic money growth. At the same time, Bank Indonesia furnished the banks with liquidity, so they could make large amounts of credits available at lower lending rates. A certain amount of credit was also directly allocated to priority sectors in conjunction with government programs.

Direct monetary control succeeded in controlling inflation and stimulating economic progress. But the end of the oil boom, followed by a world recession in the early 1980s, hit Indonesia hard. Economic growth, which had reached a high of 9.9 percent in 1980, slipped to 7.6 percent in 1982 and then to 2.3 percent in 1983. The balance of payments deficit widened from US$395 million in 1981 to $1,391 million in 1982, after having posted continuous surpluses since 1970. It was clear that although Indonesia had achieved some of its economic goals, it remained highly susceptible to world recessions and sharp economic fluctuations.

Economic Reforms in the 1980s and 1990s

The government responded in the early 1980s by instituting a set of economic reforms—known in Indonesia as "deregulation and debureaucratization"—that included a major restructuring of the financial sector.

In January 1982, the government introduced a new policy to promote nonfuel exports, which included lowering the interest rates applied to export credits, reducing export credit requirements, and increasing the number of export facilities. On March 30, 1983, the government devalued the rupiah by 28 percent[1] in an effort to boost the competitiveness of traded goods. At the same time, it reconfirmed that it would adhere to a managed floating exchange rate system, free of foreign exchange controls. It also reduced certain subsidies on food and a few other commodities, and rescheduled some large development projects to place less stress on the balance of payments.

Following these actions, the government embarked on a drastic reform of the financial sector, which was hindering the mobilization of funds and doing little to raise the efficiency and professional management of bank operations. Moreover, with the sharp drop in revenues from oil exports, it was expected that the government would confront heavy constraints in pursuing economic development. Clearly, the private sector would have to take on a much greater role in the economic development process—and that meant helping the financial institutions find a way to mobilize more funds for this group. The promotion of small- and medium-scale entrepreneurs[2] was also encouraged to reduce the productivity discrepancies among different scales of economic actors.

One of the major financial sector reforms was the October 1988 Deregulation Policy Package (PAKTO 1988), aimed at improving the functioning of the money and capital markets. Bank reserve requirements were lowered from 15 percent to 2 percent. The government switched to an indirect monetary policy, intensifying the use of Bank Indonesia Certificates and other money market securities in open market operations. Tax treatment in the money and capital markets was streamlined to equalize the competitiveness between the two markets— as well as to balance the availability of short- and long-term funds by allowing market forces to prevail. The development of venture capital, leasing, factoring, and insurance was also encouraged as a source of long-term funds.

All in all, the measures were intended to intensify competition in the financial markets, encourage new channels for financial intermediation, and reduce the cost of intermediation. It was also hoped that the higher savings would support export activities, which were expected to take off, in part thanks to several new international trade measures.

---

[1] This brought the rupiah to Rp 970 per U.S. dollar, following a 1978 devaluation of 34 percent; later, in 1986, the rupiah was devalued by another 31 percent.

[2] Also includes the nonformal sector and petty traders.

- In 1985, the government took the unprecedented step of "virtually abolishing" the Indonesian custom services—temporarily turning over customs responsibilities to the Geneva-based Societé Generale de Surveillance. Importers were freed from red tape, enabling them to reduce import costs and save time.
- In May 1986, a duty drawback facility was set up. Exporters could import their inputs duty free and directly, regardless of licensing restrictions that applied. The administration of the facility has been regarded as efficient, and the facility has substantially reduced the cost of exports, in turn boosting competitiveness.
- More recently, deregulation steps are aimed at strengthening Indonesia's ability to confront the globalization process. Indonesia is systematically abolishing nontariff barriers and gradually reducing custom duties to conform with requirements of the World Trade Organization.[3]

These reforms are naturally being taken in tandem with measures in the real sector, such as reducing restrictions on foreign direct investments, in an effort to enhance Indonesia's competitiveness in the century ahead.

Obstacles to Reform

What conclusions about economic reform can we draw from Indonesia's experience? It is obvious that the basic objective of economic reform is to gradually reduce market failures and to enable the economic system to become efficient, thereby maximizing national welfare. Thus, *economic reform is a continuous process of adjusting economic conditions* to create a macroeconomic climate—under a set of constraints relevant to the country[4]—that will be instrumental for the microeconomic decisions and activities that lead to an efficient economic system.

For Indonesia, which falls under the classification of a small and open country, the strategy is a very straightforward one: to promote an efficient economy sufficiently conditioned to a competitive international market. Naturally, in the process, Indonesia needs to confront a number of obstacles, covering political, cultural, geographical, demographic, and ethnic considerations.

---

[3]Indonesia is actively preparing itself to conform with conditions of its membership in the World Trade Organization and goals of regional economic agreements (e.g., the expected completion of the Asian Free Trade Arrangement in 2003, and the goal of free trade for developing economy members of the Asia Pacific Economic Cooperation Forum in 2020).

[4]Indonesia adopts a working definition known as the development trilogy: stability, growth, and equity, which essentially combines objectives and targets in interchangeable order.

In gearing up the Indonesian economy to reach efficiency, reform has focused on three key components: getting the prices right, making the market mechanism work, and reducing "bureaucratic costs." Let us examine these, one by one.

Getting the Prices Right

The goal of adjusting prices is to nudge especially the key prices in an economy to a level where they reflect the real value of commodities and resources exchanged.

In the past, Indonesia had subsidized key commodities, including petroleum products and basic foods such as rice, wheat, and sugar. But by reducing and to some extent eliminating the subsidies in recent years, price determination of these commodities is now left to the market. This has encouraged producers, including farmers, to produce more food staples—to some extent bringing Indonesia to the point of self-sufficiency in rice. This is a position that Indonesia had never even dreamed of, given its history over the past century of always importing rice from its South Asian neighbors.

Needless to say, eliminating subsidies is not an easy job for policymakers since it is a highly politically charged issue. Producers will welcome such a move, but consumers, who have enjoyed lower prices, will not. Thus, policymakers will need to be courageous, carefully weighing questions of political stability. For example, Indonesia's recent decision to increase the domestic fuel price is a very sensitive one—one that will not enhance the government's popularity. Nevertheless, continually subsidizing this commodity would have placed a lasting and growing burden on the budget, in turn draining resources needed for other programs.

Making the Market Mechanism Work

The goal in this area is to create an atmosphere that is conducive for the market to set prices without any intervention by the authorities. This will keep the process of developing efficient prices on the right track, in turn improving resource allocation.

Of course, this is easy to say but difficult to execute. Although everybody knows that the remedy for ailing economies is to let the market take care of itself, opposition will come from virtually all directions. First, it will come from those who are benefiting from special privileges of procuring certain commodities both for consumption and as inputs in manufacturing. Second, it will come from consumers, such as city dwellers who are used to lower prices for consumer goods, especially food staples. Clearly, the government will not be able to satisfy every-body, as there will be conflicting interests.

Indonesia's experience suggests that as long as the government holds firm, market participants will adjust to the new conditions, although of course not immediately. The government's strategy should be to eradi-cate obstacles gradually, in a sympathetic but systematic way—if neces-sary through indirect measures that will bring the market mechanism into play. Moreover, once the financial market becomes more competi-tive, it will help bring the whole economy, including the real sector, to a market-based system with minimal intervention. Efficient price deter-mination through a market mechanism is a sine qua non for enhancing the global competitiveness of Indonesian products. Competition also forces producers to place more weight on an efficient manufacturing strategy, which in turn will reduce costs and ultimately boost produc-tivity and profits. In addition, producers will be able to find a favorable niche and survive in the global market.

For Indonesia, two other special considerations have surfaced. First, the world's largest island country has had to contend with unbalanced regional conditions. For example, Eastern Indonesia has been left be-hind in certain areas of development—even sometimes in agriculture—owing to unbalanced demographic spreads (i.e., lower population). Sec-ond, some ethnic groups are still demanding government intervention in certain sectors of the economy, such as land ownership. Thus, the government needs to carefully and wisely address this issue, because if mishandled it could create a crisis that would quickly spiral out of control.

Reducing Bureaucratic Costs

This third component of reform is rather difficult to execute, but the problem is without question a source of high economic cost. It involves a nonmarket allocation of "rent" going to the institutions, as well as to the bureaucrats themselves. Thus, reform must embrace institutional re-form, including interinstitutional relations, and organizational reform within the bureaucratic system, including the supervision aspect.

Policymakers sometimes ignore the importance of reforming bureau-cracies, especially due to the fact that it takes years to succeed. But un-less institutional reforms are made, bureaucracy will hinder the process of making market mechanisms work—possibly negating the fruit of the reform itself.

Needless to say, one of the strategies is to establish an environment of discipline. This includes budget discipline, banking and monetary disci-pline, and bureaucratic discipline (e.g., relations among the various governmental agencies). Of course, it also helps if the affected bureaucratic elements understand the necessity of the reform. Indonesia's experience with reforming the customs service is a good example, underscoring that even an extreme reform can be executed smoothly with relatively little conflict, providing that everybody understands and accepts the objective.

Concluding Remarks

In sum, the Indonesian experience tells us that it is very hard to differentiate economic reforms from policy adjustment. One may say economic reform is an activist policy, while policy adjustment is reactionary, when, in fact, economic reform also involves a series of adjustments. However, it is true that the rationale behind the economic reforms may include a long-term impact, whereas the rationale behind policy adjustment may be focused on short-term considerations. Moreover, the series of adjustments to the long-term vision of reform will be necessary to remove the obstacles that policymakers encounter.

General Discussion

Economic Policy and Democracy

Basant Kapur of Singapore, picking up on Kwesi Botchwey's statement that countries would benefit economically from a stable democratic environment, suggested that the key question was not whether a democratic or authoritarian regime was needed but rather whether the country was achieving economic growth. After all, initially, South Korea and Taiwan were not democratic regimes, but their form of authoritarianism had proved quite capable of pushing through economic reforms. Moreover, some democratic regimes were riddled with corruption, while authoritarian countries such as China had managed to combine corruption and very rapid economic growth. What was needed above all were market-oriented and outward-oriented strategies that enabled systemic corruption to be reduced and business to be promoted, and studies should be undertaken to establish the best way of designing and implementing these strategies. Robert Barro had asked if it was democracy that brought about economic growth or if economic growth allowed democracy to flourish. So one might well ask if it was possible to assume that economic growth should come first and democracy second.

Dahlan Sutalaksana of Indonesia suggested that some of the sensitivity surrounding the issue stemmed from the fact that democracy was not necessarily defined the same way in every nation. If Indonesia had followed the Western-style democratic way, it would have picked Javanese as the national language in the late 1940s, as the majority of the population then spoke Javanese, and it would make Islam the national religion, as most Indonesians were Islamic. But instead, the government had opted not to establish a national religion, and the Indonesian language was developed from several regional languages (such as Malay). Although human rights issues needed to be addressed worldwide, economic growth could stimulate the process to true democracy. Thus, the answer lay in managing the country so that economic policies were good, the government was good, and the results were good.

Joseph Tsika of the Congo, however, observed that his nation, like many others, really had no choice. Because of poor economic management decisions in the past, the Congo now had to turn to the international community for help in financing growth. But the donors insisted that they would only provide financial support if the country became more democratic. Autocratic policies used to enable the Congo to mobilize everyone behind an ideal, but that was no longer possible with a democratic system.

Reacting to these remarks, *Kwesi Botchwey* offered a defense of democracy for Africa. Democratization was important for development because it affected the sustainability of reform programs and helped mobilize people at the regional and district levels. Good autocrats were fine so long as they remained good, and pursued good economic policies. But the problem was that when they ceased to be good, there was no way to get rid of them. Thus, it was important to anchor the reform process in a political environment that made it possible for the electors to get rid of the elected when they turned wayward. How this should be done, however, should be left up to the country. Moreover, countries should not rush into the democratization process and should not define democratization as a checklist of things to be done that would automatically reproduce what had happened in the Western democracies.

But should democracy be a condition of financial support? As long as the macroeconomic policy framework was good and the processes of resource mobilization and use were accountable and transparent, the minimum conditions for financial support existed to enable the donors and the adjusting country, through informal dialogue and consultation, to gradually encourage the evolution of a full-fledged democratic environment.

The problem with democracy and development in Africa, Botchwey continued, was partly the way democracy had been introduced into the development battle between donors and African countries. There was a presumption that African governments and people left on their own would not democratize, that somehow they were almost innately autocratic, and therefore, without the carrot and the stick, things would not happen. The concept of democracy was put forward, but it really meant

Western-style democracy, pure and simple. In addition, Africans had a great deal of concern about inconsistencies in Western attitudes toward democracy—inconsistencies that had sapped the moral strength of the call for democracy. There was a perception in the developing world that when the market was large and the spoils sufficiently attractive, donors found a way of turning their eyes away from obvious abuses, such as in human rights.

In response to a question from Jacob Mwanza of Zambia as to why Ghana's macroeconomic performance—often cited as a success story—had deteriorated after the democratization process had begun and governance had improved, and what that said about the links between performance, democracy, and good governance, Botchwey pointed out that before democratization, the government (even though it was not elected) had made greater use of dialogue and consultation with those involved than subsequently. In addition, starting in 1992, with the democratization of the trade union, a great deal of pressure was exerted on the government, causing the wage bill to rise to an unsustainable level. Everyone started to negotiate, negotiate, and negotiate, and everyone was engrossed in politics and winning elections. Obviously, there had to be an economic impact, and thus a price was paid for democratization. But the problems arising from democratization were being overcome, and they could be resolved through debate.

Jean-Claude Brou of Côte d'Ivoire concurred with Botchwey's emphasis on the value of dialogue and consultation among the various parties in a country. Only with such communication was it possible to stick to proper macroeconomic policies over the long term, and democracy offered a way of keeping those avenues of internal communication open. Thus, although appropriate macroeconomic policies were the sine qua non for development, the democratic process was also essential. But there was no point in comparing a country that had 200 years of democracy behind it with one that had started only 3 or 4 years ago with a special socioeconomic situation. Each country had to find its own way down that road.

On another topic, *Michael Foster* of the United Kingdom asked Sutalaksana how Indonesia, unlike many other oil producers, had managed to avoid the so-called Dutch disease—whereby the result of having a large oil sector is a loss of competitiveness of the other tradable sectors because of an overvalued exchange rate. The United Kingdom suffered from this disease in the early 1980s, and Nigeria had suffered from it over the years at a great cost. Part of the answer no doubt was keeping the exchange rate more competitive through a devaluation. But how could Indonesia achieve a real devaluation in light of the potentially adverse monetary consequences of trying to effect that?

Sutalaksana responded that fortunately Indonesia had immediately recognized the problem in the early 1980s because it had been listening to advisors and observing the experiences of other countries. What was Indonesia's solution? First, it used some of the oil proceeds to repay loans, rather than reschedule them as originally planned. Second, it took drastic measures to promote exports of non-oil goods, including the liberalization of imports of raw materials for these goods. Third, it tried to monitor imports more tightly, in part through preshipment inspections. As a result, oil and gas exports now accounted for only about 33 percent of total exports, sharply down from about 80 percent in 1982.

How to Accelerate Reform

4

Strengthening Revenue Mobilization Efforts in Sub-Saharan Africa

Peter S. Heller

IT IS WELL RECOGNIZED that an adequate noninflationary revenue mobilization effort is critical for the financing of a government's necessary social and economic expenditure obligations. Unfortunately, in sub-Saharan Africa, the tax effort in two-thirds of the countries has been disappointingly low, with tax revenue as a percent of GDP at or below 15 percent; indeed, almost one-third have ratios below 10 percent of GDP (see Table 1). Equally disturbing, many countries have witnessed a decline in their tax effort in recent years. As a result, many donors and international institutions have focused their technical assistance for Africa on strengthening revenue performance. This paper explores why revenue performance in Africa has been weak and what strategy can be adopted to remedy the problem.

Before answering these questions, five caveats should be mentioned. First, there *are* a few countries (8 out of a sample of 29) where tax efforts can be considered adequate, exceeding 20 percent. Although in a few countries this reflects a tax base that depends on the mining sector, there are other countries, notably Kenya, Seychelles, South Africa, and Zimbabwe, where the tax base is considerably more diversified—signaling what is possible in other parts of Africa.

The author expresses his gratitude to Jean-Paul Bodin, John Crotty, Liam Ebrill, James Walsh, and Howell Zee for useful comments. Of course, all views are the full responsibility of the author.

Table 1. Tax Revenue Levels in Sub-Saharan Africa Still Need a Sharp Boost
(As percent of GDP)

	1990	1991	1992	1993	1994
Benin	7.9	8.8	10.0	10.9	10.8
Botswana[1]	37.5	42.0	40.6	40.6	37.3
Burkina Faso	10.2	10.1	8.7	9.3	10.1
Cameroon[2,3,4]	11.0	10.6	11.5	11.6	8.9
Central African Republic	10.4	8.6	8.2	6.8	6.3
Chad	7.9	6.4	6.3	6.2	5.4
Congo[3]	16.0	15.9	14.7	15.5	12.7
Côte d'Ivoire	17.6	16.9	17.0	14.9	16.3
Equatorial Guinea	14.3	13.5	14.1	13.9	10.9
Gabon[3]	11.7	12.6	12.4	12.4	10.2
Gambia[2]	19.3	19.8	20.4	21.8	20.0
Ghana	10.8	12.4	10.0	12.9	16.2
Guinea-Bissau	8.0	6.5	3.9	5.0	6.5
Kenya[2]	19.5	20.1	19.8	20.0	26.0
Mali[5]	9.8	12.1	10.4	11.1	9.9
Mauritius[2,6]	22.0	22.4	20.7	19.9	19.7
Niger[5]	7.9	7.0	6.7	6.6	5.4
Nigeria[7,8]	4.4	4.7	3.9	3.6	4.4
Senegal[6,9]	14.5	15.6	15.3	13.9	12.4
Seychelles[5]	38.3	34.3	34.5	36.6	34.1
Sierra Leone[2,5]	8.6	9.6	11.6	13.3	13.6
South Africa[1]	25.1	24.0	23.8	23.2	23.9
Swaziland[1]	27.0	27.9	28.8	27.4	28.7
Tanzania[2]	12.1	14.0	14.8	11.4	13.5
Togo[5]	18.7	15.2	12.6	8.6	11.3
Uganda[6]	6.3	8.0	7.3	8.1	9.7
Zaïre[10]	9.3	4.4	2.7	3.4	2.9
Zambia	19.9	18.3	17.5	14.1	16.8
Zimbabwe[2]	30.4	30.5	33.3	27.6	26.8

Sources: IMF country documents; and staff estimates.
[1]Fiscal year beginning April 1.
[2]Fiscal year ending June 30.
[3]Non-oil tax revenue, non-oil GDP.
[4]Calendar year or fiscal year ending the calendar year.
[5]Government revenue.
[6]Budgetary central government revenue.
[7]Federal government revenue.
[8]Including inland revenue, customs and excise taxes and VAT.
[9]Fiscal year ending June 30 through 1991/92, calendar year date starting in 1992.
[10]In billions of new zaïres from 1994 onward.

Second, while this paper argues that there is a basic and practical strategy for improving the tax system, there is not a "one size fits all" tax policy regime that is appropriate in all cases. Differences in economic base, openness to trade, the degree of reliance on natural resources, the relative importance of the informal sector, administrative capacity, and the nature of the political and economic linkages to other countries would all influence what would be the appropriate tax policy and administrative regime.

Third, a government's resource mobilization efforts do not occur in a vacuum and are unlikely to be successful in an adverse political environment or in the context of a badly managed macroeconomic policy regime. Indeed, it would be difficult for even the ideal tax policy regime and the most efficient tax administration to function effectively and yield adequate revenue under such circumstances. Weak economic policies that have led to hyperinflation, stagnant or negative growth, overvalued exchange rates, and large government payments arrears erode tax bases and induce tax evasion, thus contributing to deteriorating revenues. Civil disorder, lack of political will to stem corruption, and grossly inadequate salaries weaken the capacity of many tax administrations that were once effective.

A corollary point is that strategies to strengthen tax policy and administration are likely to be more successful in the context of a sound macroeconomic policy regime and a politically supportive environment for reform. Political will is particularly vital, whether for the adoption of a simple tax system or for the establishment of an effective tax administration.

Fourth, one must be realistic in terms of the improvement in revenue ratios that can be reasonably expected to be achieved in many African countries, given the low level of development and the heavily agricultural and informal sector character of their economies.

Last, one should not forget that a high tax effort is not desirable in and of itself, but only in the context of the social benefits perceived to result from a given level and structure of public expenditure.

In what follows, I shall initially lay out the constellation of factors that have contributed to Africa's recurring weak revenue performance, and then describe the elements of a strategy that the IMF's Fiscal Affairs Department has been recommending in recent years and that has served as the basis for some progress in revenue mobilization in several African countries. Such recommendations—encompassing both policy changes and administrative reforms—typically arise during the Fiscal Affairs Department's technical assistance work and in the context of IMF program negotiations and Article IV consultations.

Reasons Behind Weak Revenue Performance

Poor revenue performance in Africa can be attributed to a number of factors. To begin with, both the number of "tax handles" and the size of the tax base with which they are associated tend to be fairly limited. This results from the fact that most sub-Saharan economies must contend with low per capita income, an income base largely derived from agriculture (of which the subsistence sector is often quite important), and manufacturing and service sectors that include a significant informal sector.

Next, most countries suffer from weaknesses in the economic policy environment or political milieu. Moreover, once such weaknesses have adversely affected an economy or dramatically reduced the administrative capacity of the tax agency, it may take a number of years, even under appropriate policies, to rebuild and restore the viability of a government's capacity for resource mobilization.

Tax policy regimes in African countries also tend to share certain features that both erode the potential for revenue mobilization and distort their impact on the efficiency of resource allocation and incentives for growth. Such features include customs duty structures characterized by an excessive number of multiple nominal tariff rates, significant dispersion in the rates of effective protection, and numerous exemptions; complicated multiple rate indirect tax systems applied to only a limited number of sectors and resulting in significant cascading; enterprise income taxes limited to the formal sector and subject to extensive tax incentive provisions; personal income taxes that are almost exclusively applied to wage incomes in the formal/government sector and that are subject to high average and marginal tax rates; and export taxes that, although constituting an alternative approach for taxing the agricultural sector, give rise to significant resource allocational distortions.

Exemptions in particular weaken the tax and tariff system. In some countries, more than half of imports and domestic economic activity is exempt, reflecting generous investment codes, corruption, abuses of the system by suppliers of exempted enterprises, loose controls over the granting of exemptions by government agencies, and special regimes for nongovernmental organizations (NGOs), externally financed government projects, and diplomatic personnel. Tax exemptions for agricultural inputs have also been used by African governments as a way of fostering agricultural productivity.

Finally, weaknesses in tax and customs administration go a long way in explaining why it has proven difficult to improve the revenue performance of many African countries. Factors *systemic* to a country's public administration are obviously important, including overstaffing, very low salaries, poor training, inadequate supplies and materials, lack of equipment and vehicles, limited or inappropriate computerization, and poor management practices.[1] Deficiencies in the tax policy regime also beget administrative weaknesses. High tax rates, multiple exemptions,

---

[1]Poor management practices are often exemplified by ill-defined work priorities, a lack of effective supervision of staff, an absence of documented procedures, limited coordination across departmental operations, and ineffective implementation of reform measures.

and diffuse authority over the granting of exemptions can encourage evasion as well as create inducements for corruption and rent seeking among low-paid tax officials. The politicization of customs organizations is common.

In addition to a lack of political will to support vigorous tax collection efforts, specific weaknesses in the organization of tax and customs administrations and unprioritized approaches for assessment, collection, audit, and valuation are also common. For example, current tax collection procedures in much of francophone Africa consume large administrative resources and yet effectively involve lengthy delays between the filing of a tax return and the assessment and payment of the tax liability by a taxpayer. Collection responsibilities are often dispersed between separate administrations, creating additional opportunities for corrupt practices. Approaches to auditing in many countries are highly inefficient and involve lengthy delays and frequent legal proceedings; in general, there is little incentive for compliance by taxpayers. Customs administrations are similarly hampered by an excessive number of regulations and exemptions; complicated tariff structures; poor and haphazard controls on the transit, clearance, and bonding of imports; deficient valuation procedures (leading to cases of both under- and overinvoicing); inadequate audit procedures;[2] negligible penalties for misrepresentation; and significant payment arrears.

Strategies for Strengthening Revenue Mobilization Efforts

A review of the recent experience with tax and customs policy and administrative reform in sub-Saharan Africa[3] suggests much activity, albeit with many initiatives still at a very early stage of implementation. For a few countries, reform has been pursued with sufficient resolve to raise revenue shares, albeit often from low levels (notably Benin, Ghana, Kenya, and Uganda).[4] I start with the thrust of the tax policy advice that

---

[2]Typically, a customs administration will undertake the most superficial checks on *all* imported goods rather than well-targeted selective inspections and post-clearance audits.

[3]In what follows, I have drawn upon the results of a recent (1995) joint IMF–Government of France Symposium on "Major Government Finance Problems Facing the Countries of French-Speaking Africa."

[4]Obviously, such policy actions, whether preliminary or sustained, only explain part of revenue developments in the region. For example, in Francophone Africa, the devaluation of early 1994 played an important role in arresting the growing deterioration of revenue shares, although one could argue that better results were achieved by the countries that had strengthened their tax administration systems (e.g., Benin and Gabon) prior to the devaluation, as this allowed them to benefit more fully from the devaluation.

the Fiscal Affairs Department offers in its technical assistance program, followed by an examination of the recommended strategies for reforming tax and customs administrations.

Strategies for Tax Reform

When a country evaluates the appropriate tax policy regime, given its resource mobilization objectives, key considerations include the minimization of resource allocational distortions, the capacity of the tax administration, the government's distributional objectives, and the extent to which the government is committed to regional tax and tariff harmonization objectives. While these factors may result in different strategies across countries, a number of common elements would appear appropriate for Africa and are often recommended by the Fiscal Affairs Department in its technical assistance work.

Typically, the advice includes keeping tax and tariff rates low, broadening the tax base as much as possible, minimizing the number of exemptions and incentives, reducing reliance on international trade taxes, and simplifying the tax system to facilitate both administration and taxpayer compliance. For countries embarking on trade liberalization, increased reliance on broad-based consumption taxes—specifically, a simple value–added tax (VAT)—becomes necessary. The use of excises should be limited to those commodities for which distributional or external considerations argue for tax instruments to discourage consumption or excessive exploitation of resources. Other elements of reform include a strengthening of the schedular income tax system and a simplification of the approach to taxing small businesses (including introducing a form of income tax withholding at the import stage and reducing the minimum profit tax). At times, the tradeoff between the desirability of policy reforms and administrative simplicity would need to be considered (e.g., with respect to export taxation).

In laying out these "common elements" of policy, it is useful to recall the words of my colleague, Milka Casanegra, that "in Africa, tax administration *is* tax policy!" While this is certainly not the whole story, this admonition does remind us of the administrative considerations that, in the case of the sub-Saharan countries, point to the desirability of a relatively simple tax policy regime. For example, while we may be hesitant to recommend a schedular tax system in an industrial country (for which we would normally prefer taxation on a global base), it is likely to be the appropriate approach for a sub-Saharan country, reflecting the common administrative constraints that prevail. What are these common elements? They include the following.

Reduce and control exemptions.[5] This requires, first and foremost, strong political will from the highest level of government. Customs and tax laws and regulations should be revised to limit severely the scope for possible exemptions, including repealing all tax waiver provisions in investment codes (replacing them with ordinary legal provisions in the tax and customs codes); eliminating exemptions on all unidentifiable fungibles (fuels), primary commodities, consumer goods, and spare parts; setting fixed limits on the time period over which exemptions are available (no more than four years), and forbidding the renewal of exemptions. For oil exporters, all tax waivers for subcontracting should be eliminated (with a provision made for exporters to seek a refund for indirect taxes paid by subcontractors on inputs). Exemptions for NGOs should be tightly controlled and, where possible, restricted to specific quantities of certain items (cars, personal effects) for limited periods. Abuses in the use of diplomatic tax exemptions should be monitored.

Normally, countries will also need to revise the legal procedures for granting exemptions and the criteria used in evaluating the desirability of an exemption. In particular, tax exemptions should be issued *only* by the minister of finance (with limits on delegating decision-making within the ministry). A single, transparent, centralized procedure would need to be introduced for granting any exemptions (including requiring ministries to provide estimates of the loss in duty and revenue implied by granting exemptions).[6] Budgetary procedures may also need to be revised to ensure that government ministries are budgeted on a tax- and duty-inclusive basis, and policymakers may need to renegotiate exemptions for project or program imports with donors.[7]

Move to a simplified form of the VAT. We believe that the VAT is a revenue instrument that can generate significant revenues while also being nondistortive in terms of its resource allocational effects. It has been introduced in a number of African countries, and in recent years several of these—notably Benin, Burkina Faso, Gabon, and Zambia—have implemented reforms to strengthen its efficiency. Successful implementation requires that the legislation be kept simple. In particular, it is preferable to have only one rate (other than for zero-rated goods); as broad a

---

[5]Such a policy can contribute both to an increase in revenues and a lower customs tariff rate.

[6]Tanzania is an example of a country where efforts are being made to make the procedures for granting exemptions more transparent.

[7]A highly successful approach to limit abuses of exemptions associated with externally financed projects is for the government to negotiate, ex ante, the magnitude of the import duty exemption associated with a project. The contractor would then pay the import duty on all project inputs using a predetermined credit voucher, based on the ex ante calculation of the exempted duties.

tax base as possible (with only limited exemptions, such as on the most essential consumer goods and services); a zero rate applied only to exports; and a turnover threshold that ensures that the domestic VAT is applied to the larger taxpaying enterprises, which are fewer, that are capable of meeting the legal and reporting obligations consistent with a country's administrative capacity.[8] Smaller enterprises, who may indirectly end up paying VAT on their purchases of inputs, have the option of registering for the VAT and receiving credits.

Adoption of a VAT can normally be phased in over a period of 12–18 months, taking account of the information and training needs of both taxpayers and the tax administration. VAT administrative reforms should embody the recommendations discussed above.[9]

Simplify the approach to taxing small enterprises. Taxation of this sector cannot be ignored if one is to prevent evasion through the hiding of large taxpayer transactions through informal sector units and limit the competitive distortions that would arise if only the formal sector were taxed. Yet the administration of taxes on small enterprises is often unsatisfactory in many African countries. In the French system, the "forfait" system is typically used, requiring negotiation with each enterprise to determine tax liabilities under the different taxes applicable to enterprises (e.g., VAT, turnover tax, profit tax, or annual license fee). Such an approach tends to be costly to administer, low in revenue yield, and susceptible to collusion between the taxpayer and tax official negotiating the forfait level.

Several alternative approaches to the taxation of small enterprises and the self-employed are being tried in a number of African countries (notably Benin and Côte d'Ivoire). One is the introduction of a single business tax, which would constitute a minimum level of taxation. Such a tax is levied on a proportional basis, usually at a low rate (1–2 percent), on the rent paid by an enterprise (e.g., as in Benin); alternatively, the tax is levied on the enterprise's turnover (e.g., in Niger and Côte d'Ivoire). A further variant is Uganda's commercial transactions levy, which is a tax on services that is applied on a minimum presumptive basis. Such taxes can initially be administered through "community policing" techniques (e.g., in Benin).

---

[8] While some countries have advocated a second, reduced rate for basic consumer goods, this complicates the administration of the VAT, making it more costly for both taxpayers and tax departments. It also opens the door to political pressures to change the rates for any given good.

[9] Specifically, this would include a special unit for large enterprises, introduction of single identification numbers, computerization of the taxpayer master file, a policy of tax cross-checking and targeted field audits, and the combining of filing, payment, and refund procedures within the tax administration.

A schedular withholding tax system can also be used as a means of ensuring at least minimal income tax payments by small enterprises or the self-employed. For example, large enterprises and government agencies can be required to withhold a certain share of their payments to professionals or individual contractors, again at a low proportional withholding tax rate. Similarly, businesses may be required to pay a 3–5 percent withholding tax on imports, which would be creditable only against the income tax. (e.g., in Benin, Burkina Faso, and Togo).

The Fiscal Affairs Department also typically recommends a significant reduction in the so-called "minimum profit taxes." Presently, some francophone countries levy such a tax on gross turnover, usually at a rate of 4–5 percent. Although creditable against the income or profit tax, such a tax rate would appear too high, particularly since the credit would be unavailable to loss-making enterprises.

Improve the current schedular income tax system. Most African countries rely on a schedular income tax applied to wage and salary income for employees in the formal sector. Such a tax usually works well and facilitates a reasonably buoyant and equitable basis for generating income tax revenues. Problems typically emerge when policymakers fail to adjust tax rate brackets during periods of inflation, and when there are excessively detailed rate schedules, complicated exemption formulas, and an unduly high top marginal tax rate. Also, many countries fail to apply a schedular tax to interest and dividend income. While such an approach is decidedly second best to a progressive global income tax for achieving equity objectives, schedular taxes on capital income sources—namely, a proportional withholding tax on capital source income—are relatively easy to administer and would establish a basic measure of equity in a tax system.[10]

Reduce reliance on export taxation. While there may be some economic justification for export taxes in a limited number of circumstances (e.g., monopolies or dominant producers), in general, export taxes are simply used to compensate for the ineffectiveness of other forms of taxing agricultural income. This is a problem because export taxes not only hold the potential to adversely affect domestic production but also subsidize domestic consumption of exportables and contribute to a poor allocation of resources, particularly among various crops. Thus, the Fiscal Affairs Department generally recommends reducing effective export tax rates (mitigating the negative effects on production), deducting export duties from the income tax payable by individuals and corporations,

---

[10]Again, while a global income tax may allow for greater progressivity, if poorly administered and subject to significant delays and delinquencies, it may, in practice, be counterproductive in terms of achieving equity objectives.

eliminating export taxes on products for which domestic demand is
strong, and substituting an income tax if only one or a few enterprises
produce or market a product.

Rely on an integrated rather than a piecemeal approach. It is important
to recognize the links between the various elements of a tax reform
strategy. Reforming customs duties will be difficult if the policy regime
for other domestic consumption taxes (excises, sales tax/VAT) is in dis-
array. Similarly, removing direct tax incentives is often easier to achieve
if accompanied by a reform of the structure of the enterprise income
tax.

Core Strategy for Strengthening Tax Administration

Strengthening the efficiency of the tax collection effort is important
for enhancing revenue mobilization, minimizing the allocative distortions required to achieve revenue objectives, and achieving greater ver-
tical and horizontal equity among taxpayers. The starting point is a
recognition of the basic realities of many African countries in terms of
(1) the limited number of enterprises that are likely to be liable for a significant amount of taxes (other than the mass of civil servants, for whom
tax withholding by the government is administratively simple) and
(2) the small number of administrative points at which tax and tariff collections are likely to be most significant and productive.[11] This situation
reflects the importance of imports in these economies and the limited
size of the formal manufacturing sector. What would an effective strategy entail? The advice of the Fiscal Affairs Department in this area prin-
cipally focuses on strengthening collections and audit functions.

- Consistent with reforms in the tax policy regime, the *focus should
mainly be on the larger taxpaying units in the economy.* This reflects the reality that in most African countries, only a small number of taxpayers
account for the bulk of taxes due (from corporate income taxes, excises,
and sales taxes).[12] Central to the strategy would be the *establishment of a
large enterprise collection and audit unit.* In a system based on the self-
assessment approach (see below), such an administrative unit would be

---

[11]In practice, this means a significant centralization of controls over the major taxpayers in
a country and, where necessary, the transfer of responsibility for those taxpayers from regional
and municipal offices of the tax administration. Also, as part of the strategy, lower priority is
accorded to collection of taxes such as the property tax, which normally generate minimal revenues to the national government.

[12]In a typical African country of population 5–10 million, there are normally an average
1,000–2,000 enterprises of significant size, with only a small number accounting for the bulk
of receipts.

expected to focus its energies forcefully on sending reminders and imposing penalties on the most important delinquent taxpayers (in terms of potential revenue losses).[13] However, this approach would also need to be complemented by a strategy to ensure the *minimal* taxation of smaller enterprises, particularly in the informal sector (see below), where activity levels are below the threshold for which formal registration and tax filing would be required.

• *For legal taxpaying units (e.g., enterprises), there should be a shift toward a system of self-assessment and self-payment of taxes.* Specifically, enterprises would be expected to calculate the taxes that they owe and then make the payment at the same time as they file their returns. One tax office would be responsible for both receipt of the tax return and the tax payment. This departs from existing tax assessment procedures commonly applied to direct taxes, whereby tax administrators first review and calculate tax assessments for each taxpaying enterprise, then notify it as to its outstanding tax liability—but payments are made to a completely different government agency. In fact, a notice of tax assessment should be issued only when an audit suggests a need for additional payments.

• *Only one organization should have the responsibility for collecting tax filings and payments* (in contrast to the divided responsibilities across separate administrations found in many African countries). Such a reform would significantly increase efficiency, reduce opportunities for embezzlement and rent seeking, and provide a clearer bureaucratic assignment of responsibility for revenue collections.

• To facilitate self-assessment, there should be *a simplification of tax forms.*

• *Taxpayer identification numbers should be assigned,* with the initial focus being on large taxpayer units, but with later extensions to the rest of the business sector and the self-employed.[14] Eventually, such identification numbers would also be assigned to individuals.

• *Audits should be targeted, focused on only one tax, and covering only a short time period.* This would contrast with prevailing practices, which involve general and typically very lengthy audits that examine tax returns spanning several years and encompassing all taxes for which an enterprise is liable. Audits should normally be triggered by the discovery of an inconsistency or discrepancy in the tax return and/or of a failure by a large enterprise to file. A general audit should be undertaken only in

---

[13]Zambia is an example of a country where concerted efforts by the tax administration have resulted in the collection of significant tax arrears.

[14]In Uganda, the assignment of unique taxpayer identification numbers to all taxpayers has provided the foundation for the introduction of the VAT and for the modernization of tax administration procedures.

cases of serious and repeated fraud, as might be detected during targeted audits, and would be carried out by a small, carefully selected team of properly trained experts.

- *Procedures should be gradually computerized,* but with the caveat that the sequenced introduction of well-specified computerization modules would be linked to the achievement of streamlined procedures and the issuance of taxpayer identification numbers. Initially, the focus should be on establishing the taxpayer master file and issuing monthly reminders to delinquent taxpayers. Subsequently, modules could be developed to detect inconsistencies and to cross-check returns, across taxpayer units and/or against information from customs.

Organizational reforms are also critical, although sometimes the solutions are aimed at the tax or customs administration alone, when the problems affect the public sector more generally. For example, one would wish to see a rationalization of staffing, coupled with an initiative to bring compensation levels closer to those found in the private sector. A strategy for training and human resource development would also be essential.

Reforms more specific to the problems of a tax and customs administration normally involve the provision of increased institutional autonomy, a revamping of the organizational structure of the tax collections unit, the issuance of an ethics code, and the imposition of adequate penalties for cases of malfeasance. In recent years, many countries— Kenya, Uganda, Zambia, and, in the near future, South Africa—have even taken the step of establishing autonomous revenue authorities. Separating the revenue authority from the civil service is expected to facilitate greater efficiency (through economies of scale in revenue collection, greater insulation from political pressures, reduced duplication of efforts, and an enhanced capacity for cross-checking capabilities), obtain a higher quality staff (as the authority would be able to set competitive salary scales and undertake employment rationalization policies), and secure an independent source of funding (typically determined as a fixed percentage of revenue collections). It will be interesting to see if these greater efficiencies can be achieved.

Strategies for Strengthening Customs Administration

Liberalization of trade has become a central theme of structural adjustment throughout the world. Africa is no exception. Trade liberalization normally entails a reduction in average tariff rates and a shift of resource mobilization efforts toward consumption-based taxes. Ironically, these trends accentuate the importance of a strengthened customs administration in Africa, since for virtually all countries it would be at the point of entry to the country that *all* forms of taxation on imported goods (be it customs duties, VAT, or an excise) would be levied or exemptions granted.[15] Similarly, for exports, any VAT rebates associated with exports would need to be initiated at this point. Reducing the cost and uncertainty associated with customs clearance operations will also be critical for the competitiveness of importers and exporters. Strengthening the quality of data on the value and quantity of trade will continue to be vital as an input to the macroeconomic policy formulation process. Thus, a strengthening of customs control, valuation, and data collection procedures at the point of entry of imports is now, more than ever, critical for revenue mobilization in Africa.

As with tax administration, efforts to strengthen the customs administration must inevitably focus on details, procedures, and organizational processes. Reforms must be prioritized in terms of those key stages in the process where the revenue consequences of inefficiencies will be the largest; the emphasis should be on simplification, rationalization, and, where relevant, computerization.[16] The sequencing of reforms must also reflect the early introduction of measures that do not require a lengthy time for preparation relative to those for which significant advance planning and training are required. Beyond the types of organizational reforms discussed above, the elements of a customs reform strategy should focus on the following.

• *Simplification and rationalization of tariffs* (lowering the maximum tariff level and reducing the number of rates to no more than three), as well as of the associated customs laws and regulations. This would also include *eliminating most import duty exemptions.* While these are obviously more of the nature of policy reforms (as noted above), a simplification initiative should also be recognized as a prerequisite for increased administrative efficiency;

• *Strengthening of customs procedures,* based on risk assessment and selective controls targeted at high risk goods and enterprises. Import pro-

---

[15]The more advanced approaches to levying duties or taxes that are now being developed in the European Union (e.g., at nonborder points) are not likely to be feasible in Africa for the foreseeable future.

[16]In some countries, preshipment inspection services provided by private agencies (on a fee for service basis) have been introduced in the expectation that they will generate significant revenue increases in the short term (in advance of the implementation of major customs administration reforms). However, such revenue increases are rarely achieved in that sort of time frame unless the authorities are strongly committed to these arrangements. Preshipment inspection arrangements should be considered as temporary measures to be phased out within a two- to three-year period when a comprehensive customs administration reform program has been implemented. Preshipment inspection arrangements also need to be carefully implemented and supervised by the authorities to ensure that they achieve their intended objectives.

cessing is the first and most important procedure to be reformed, with the emphasis on internationally accepted standards, codings, and forms. The procedures should be designed to (1) ensure that all goods are reported and placed under customs controls; (2) process import declarations on the principle of self-assessment; (3) reduce the number of processing steps to a minimum; (4) introduce selective, effective goods inspection; (5) release goods from customs controls in the least amount of time possible; (6) ensure that the correct amount of revenue is paid and deposited in the government account; and (7) ensure that information is provided for the timely reporting of trade statistics. Export processing is the next priority for reform, particularly for countries with a VAT, as controls should be kept to a minimum.

• *Introduction of procedures for verifying values declared for customs purposes,* both at time of release of the goods from customs control and, selectively, on a postrelease review basis. Information systems—both manual and electronic—are required to support valuation review (this may require consideration of the use of preshipment inspection in certain cases). Improving valuation controls is particularly important because, as a result of the Uruguay Round trade negotiations, all countries that are members of the World Trade Organization have five years to implement the GATT Valuation Agreement. In the past, most African countries did not use the GATT Agreement and considerable effort will be required to introduce new procedures and train staff to administer it effectively.

• *Introduction of effective postclearance review.* This approach is particularly useful to support control of valuation, tariff classification, exemptions, drawback, and origin. These reviews should be targeted based on risk. For example, goods claiming an exemption or a zero rate may be misclassified, and goods with a high rate may be undervalued.

To support the reform strategy, customs administrations will have to introduce changes in the computer systems, organization, management, recruitment and training, and service. For example, cooperation between customs and tax offices must be improved (e.g., customs should use the taxpayer identification number from the tax department). Service must be improved not only to support quick release of goods from customs control but also to process legitimate drawback claims for exporters in a timely manner.

Concluding Remarks

This paper has argued that, with political will, African countries can strengthen their revenue mobilization efforts, despite the weak prevailing economic conditions and the heavily agricultural and informal sector character of their economies. This is not a theoretical argument. Many of the individual reforms advocated above are in the process of being implemented by many African countries as part of their IMF-supported adjustment programs. On a piecemeal basis, these reforms are beginning to bear fruit. More important, in those few countries where the authorities have been willing to implement these strategies on a comprehensive basis—notably, Benin, Burkina Faso, Gabon, and Uganda—we are observing significant improvement in their revenue mobilization efforts. However, one must also recognize the limits to what can be achieved and the serious revenue constraint that is likely to continue to burden the budgets of many African countries.

Comments

Shahid Yusuf

Peter Heller has done an excellent job of defining the challenges that African countries face in mobilizing tax revenues. He has also nicely encapsulated the IMF's latest thinking on tax reform.

What I would like to do is to comment both on the challenge of raising tax revenues and on the recommendations—taking the perspective of East and Southeast Asian countries during the 1970s when, I think, their economies more closely approximated those of African countries. However, before I do that, I would like to say a word or two about tax ratios.

In his paper, Heller notes that tax effort in his sample of 29 sub-Saharan African countries has been disappointing—below 15 percent of GDP for two-thirds of the total. He also notes that in almost one-third of the countries, the ratio has been less than 10 percent. This performance is certainly disappointing. However, if one enlarges the sample to include the remaining 13 countries of sub-Saharan Africa, the picture changes somewhat. Averages for 1990–94, derived from the IMF's Economic Trends in Africa database, show that 7 of these countries had tax/GDP ratios of greater than 15 percent and only 3 (Rwanda, Madagascar, and São Tomé) were at 10 percent or below.

How does Africa compare with East and Southeast Asia? The average unweighted revenue/GDP ratio for 42 African countries was in the 17 percent plus range during 1994, a modest increase over the average for 1980–84. This is just slightly below the 18 percent figure for East and Southeast Asian countries in the 1970s. Moreover, in the early 1990s, at least 18 of the 42 sub-Saharan African countries had ratios that were equal to—or exceeded—the average for East Asian countries in the 1970s and even in the 1980s. In fact, if one takes Asia as a whole and not just Southeast and East Asia, a paper by Burgess and Stern,[1] using IMF data, shows that the average tax/GDP ratio for Asia in 1989 was 15 percent, which is less than the average for Africa in the early 1990s.

If we were to compute indices of tax effort using per capita GDP, the structure of the economy, the volume of trade, the size of the informal economy and so forth, which Heller does not do, my sense is that

---

[1]Robin Burgess and Nicholas Stern, "Taxation and Development," *Journal of Economic Literature,* Vol. 31 (June 1993), pp. 762–826.

African countries would compare quite favorably with their Asian counterparts, whether in the 1970s or even the first half of the 1980s.

Let me turn now to the structure of taxation. It is certainly true that the average African country derives much more revenue from trade taxes than the average Asian country, about 30 percent in 1986–92 as against 18 percent in Asian comparators. And to some degree, I think this is unavoidable. But the share of direct taxes and indirect taxes in total revenue is broadly similar.

Furthermore, East Asian countries in the 1970s and early 1980s had tax systems that suffered from many of the same distortions and exemptions that one finds in Africa. Whether you look at South Korea or Japan in the 1970s, you have many of the same kinds of problems that we note in the African countries.

The problems of excessively high rates and of too many bands and exemptions also existed in many of the East Asian countries. So here again the difference between African countries and fast-growing East Asian countries is not particularly stark.

Much like East Asian countries in the early 1980s, many African countries have embarked upon serious tax reforms, assisted by multilateral agencies, and Heller has talked about those. In the countries of East and Southern Africa that I know best, the recommendations he proposes are being put into effect. The tariff structure is being simplified and rates lowered. Income tax rates are being cut, and the number of bands is being reduced. Several countries have introduced value-added taxes and begun using presumptive taxes based on either standard or estimated assessments. And a few countries have set up revenue boards to improve tax administration.

So change is occurring, and it follows a pattern that emerged in East Asia only about ten years ago. For instance, if you take the tax reform process in South Korea, it starts around the late 1970s but only gathers steam in the first half of the 1980s. Likewise, in Indonesia, tax reform was implemented between 1983 and 1986. No doubt African countries could usefully accelerate the implementation of new tax measures, but it is encouraging to see that reform is being actively pursued by a large number of countries.

Let me turn now to another aspect of government resource mobilization, which is the level of public savings. What is significant about East Asia's experience to me is not so much the tax/GDP ratio and revenue effort, but the level of public saving. Most East and Southeast Asian countries were able to raise national savings by several percentage points of GDP through public savings, and the strong correlation that exists between savings rates and growth would suggest that this effort made a substantial contribution to development. For instance, public savings in the late 1970s in East Asian countries ranged from about 1.3 percent of GDP in Thailand to over 8 percent of GDP in Taiwan Province of China.

Public sector savings were the result of careful expenditure management, especially the control over administrative expenditures and subsidies to the parastatal sector. Thus, expenditure management, rather than extraordinary tax effort, was one of the factors responsible for the growth performance of East Asian countries. Expenditure management also ensured that governments gave the requisite emphasis to social sectors and infrastructure building and ensured macroeconomic stability.

African countries, even those with high tax/GDP ratios, are often less successful in containing expenditures and generating public savings. On average, they provide, for instance, 2 to 5 percent of GDP in subsidies to parastatals, and their administrative outlay tends to be high. It is in this regard that there are lessons to be learned from East Asia.

Finally, tax administration in East Asian countries is, and was, much more effective than in African countries for the reasons that Heller has given, and taxpayer compliance has been significantly higher. I tend to give a little more weight to voluntary taxpayer compliance than to tax laws and the machinery of collection.

In East Asia, taxpayer compliance, though far from perfect, as we well know, is greater than in Africa because states are better equipped institutionally to enforce penalties on evaders. Thus, the cost of evasion in East Asia is higher. Perhaps more important is the ability of the state to deliver goods and services so that, on balance, taxpayers feel that their dues are well spent and show a greater readiness to pay taxes.

To summarize, my three main points are as follows.

First, on average, tax/GDP ratios in Africa are comparable to those of East Asian countries in the 1970s. In terms of tax structure and exemptions, East Asia only began introducing significant reforms in the early to mid-1980s, and Africa is following with a decade's lag.

Second, East Asia does provide significant lessons on the control of current expenditures and the generation of public savings. This might be a higher priority for many African countries than increased tax revenues, which do introduce distortions, as Heller mentioned.

Third, revenue raising in East Asia has been aided by the enforcement capacity of the state, the political commitment to this, and the state's ability to deliver on the promises of development.

5

Financial Reform in Central Asia: Lessons from the Kyrgyz Republic

Tetsuji Tanaka

BEFORE WE CAN DECIDE whether or not the financial reform experience of a Central Asian country can be of some help to the structural reform of an African economy, we must understand the differences between the basic conditions prevailing in the Central Asian countries and those in African countries. Noteworthy in this context is that the Central Asian countries, which became independent from the former Soviet Union in 1991, already had an established socialist economic structure, and thus we cannot say that they had to develop their economies from scratch.

Even so, the Central Asian economies have been faced with two challenges: one has been to transform themselves from centrally managed economies to market-oriented ones; and the second, much like developing countries striving for a market-oriented economy, has been to achieve a take-off of their economies. In my remarks today, I would like to focus on the Kyrgyz Republic's experience with financial reform. As you perhaps know, I served as Special Economic Advisor to President Akaev of the Kyrgyz Republic and also as General Advisor to the National Bank, which is the central bank of the Kyrgyz Republic, from 1993 to 1995. For the first year, I was dispatched under the auspices of the IMF.

Reform of the Financial System

Under the monobanking system of socialist economies, national banks served only as a distributor of public funds—not providing the financial services so necessary for a market economy. Since a financial system provides a critical underpinning for a market economy, the government and central bank should be responsible for providing it.

In the Kyrgyz Republic, President Akaev and the Governor of the National Bank have been most eager to accomplish the transition to a market-oriented economy and thus have actively promoted various financial reform measures based on the recommendations of the IMF and World Bank. This type of initiative and leadership of senior government officials is essential if countries hope to succeed in reforming the financial system. What has been accomplished so far? Let me tell you of the achievements to date.

• Introduction of a two-tier banking system. In 1991, the Kyrgyz branch of Gosbank became the central bank of the Kyrgyz Republic following a change in the organizational structure of Gosbank of the USSR, and a two-tier banking system—a central bank and commercial bank sector—was introduced.

• Enactment of banking laws. In December 1992, the "Law on the National Bank" and the "Law of Bank and Banking Activities" were enacted. Based on these laws, 21 commercial banks were subsequently established. (In addition to the central bank, there are currently 18 commercial banks.) Three of these commercial banks, which were formerly national banks—the Agricultural Bank (Agroprombank),[1] the Industrial Bank (Promstroibank), and the AKB Kyrgyzstan—account for 80 percent of total assets. Four of these banks are joint ventures with foreign capital.

• Introduction of monetary policy measures. The National Bank is responsible for monetary policy and banking supervision and regulation. Within a short period, it had put in place credit auctions, a Lombard credit facility, emergency credit, treasury bill auctions, reserve requirements, and foreign exchange operations. In some cases, however, such monetary policy measures have not worked well because commercial banks have been short of funds and financial markets are still undeveloped.

• Issuance of national currency. To avoid the adverse influence from the fluctuation of the ruble and to establish an independent financial system, the central bank issued a national currency, the som, in May 1993, ahead of other Central Asian countries. Although the exchange rate was initially 4 som per U.S. dollar, it depreciated to 12 som per dollar at one time, before stabilizing at about 10 in May 1996.

• Establishment of a securities exchange system. In August 1994, the Coupon Trading Center was established to deal in coupons issued to

---

[1] Agroprombank was suspended in 1996.

promote privatization and, in May 1995, a stock exchange was established—although, to date, fewer than ten companies have listed their stocks.

Another major challenge for the Kyrgyz Republic will be to organize a payment system, as currently it takes about one week to remit funds domestically from one bank to another by mail. The financial authorities plan to establish an electronic funds transfer system. But first they are promoting a clearinghouse project as a short-term plan, and then they will embark on a gross settlement system project in which all financial institutions will participate. Though these projects face some difficulties, such as a shortage of expert staff and funds, the Japanese government and the European Bank for Reconstruction and Development are providing support.

The government must also contend with the commercial banks' large amount of nonperforming loans, mainly to former national companies as a heritage of the former Soviet Union. Such loans should be written off for a while, but that practice has been temporarily suspended and instead the banks are being asked to distinguish such loans from newly extended loans. According to the recent classification, loan losses are 20 percent of total loans, and if substandard and doubtful loans are added, the figure is 90 percent. To write off such nonperforming loans, the World Bank has implemented the PESAC plan (Privatization and Enterprise Sector Adjustment Credit, worth $60 million, in 1994) for national companies in the red and the FINSAC plan (Financial Sector Adjustment Credit, for $15 million, in 1995)—although I think neither will be easy to finalize.

Shock Therapy and Effects

For the economy as a whole—which has been suffering from economic stagnation and accelerated inflation—the Kyrgyz government agreed in 1993 to promote rapid privatization and conduct a tight fiscal and monetary policy on condition that the IMF extend a standby credit and provide an arrangement under the systemic transformation facility (STF). Keeping to its end of the bargain, the central bank restrained lending to commercial banks, so much so that commercial banks fell short of funds and banknotes, even for the payment of salaries. In a country where bank deposits are few and small and the financial market is not developed, tight control of money supply may directly affect cash flow.

As a result of such consistent shock therapy, hyperinflation, which had reached 1,300 percent a year in 1993, was brought down to 32 percent in 1995, and the som has been fluctuating at about 10 per U.S. dollar for the last two years. At the 1995 Annual Meetings of the IMF and the World Bank, this achievement was highly praised as a model for the Commonwealth of Independent States. I can conclude that such shock therapy contributed to the end of hyperinflation and the stability of the som at home and abroad.

However, funds for long-term plant and equipment investment to increase production have become scarce due to high interest rates and a liquidity crunch, GDP in 1995 dropped to less than 50 percent of the pre-independence level, and living standards have worsened considerably. Deciding when to stop shock therapy and introduce fiscal and monetary policy to boost production requires care and tact, and countries must take into account the level of accumulated capital, the maturity of market participants, and the stage of market development.

Necessity of Government Intervention

Despite all the steps that the Kyrgyz Republic has taken in recent years on the financial front, I cannot conclude that it has made much progress. First, the financial market is still very rudimentary; large banks that were formerly national banks take a cautious lending attitude or are even reluctant to extend loans given their large amount of nonperforming loans, while smaller banks are short of funds and lack measures to manage credit risk. Second, only three or four banks are even equipped to handle foreign exchange business. Third, rapid liberalization and privatization have resulted in the stagnation of production and chaotic living conditions. Fourth, persistent tight monetary policy has resulted in the shrinkage of plant and equipment investment. Fifth, the reduction of the import tariff to 10 percent has increased the degree of dependence on imported consumption goods from 40 percent before independence to 80 percent at present. And sixth, foreign currency reserves are being depleted.

What can be done? In this instance, the experiences of Japan and East Asian countries, which also had to embark on reform with scarce accumulated capital, may serve as a good reference point for Central Asian countries. One key to their success was channeling public funds to the market and letting the government set priorities for distributing the funds.

In deciding the degree of market intervention and commitment by the government, we should consider various factors, including the stage of development of individual national economies, the number of market participants, the degree of market maturity, the market practices, and history, culture, and religion. In this context, it is worth noting that in Uzbekistan, which introduced relatively moderate shock therapy, production did not stagnate compared with the Kyrgyz Republic, because moderate shock therapy did not completely harm the management of production.

However, once a market matures, the government should refrain from intervening as much as possible. Accordingly, the laws and guidelines related to economic activities in a developing market should be effective for a limited period.

The Spirit of Capitalism and the Manas Spirit

There is no question in my mind that historical and cultural conditions influence both the possibility of a shift toward a market economy and the pace of reform. It is said that ethics and a philosophy that includes asceticism are required to operate a capitalist market economy. According to German sociologist and economist Max Weber, capitalism in Europe at the end of the 19th century was supported by Protestant ethics. With respect to Japan and East Asian countries, some say that Confucianism has played an equivalent role. Although Confucianism helped maintain strong national power in the feudal era, which held back the establishment of a modern state, it can be said that on the level of individuals and families, Confucianism has nurtured the necessary stoicism and desire to abide by contracts. In the Kyrgyz Republic, there is a long folk epic of 500,000 lines called *Manas Epoth,* which extols such virtues as diligence, saving, abiding by contracts, and service to the community. I expect the Manas spirit to be in the forefront of ethics in the Kyrgyz Republic.

A market participant must also be "ascetic"—laying aside his own interests—and "fair" from a social point of view. This is especially applicable to technocrats in charge of economic and financial matters since they lead the market. They should not attach too much importance to the interests of particular groups, be they political, regional, tribal, or family. Along this line, it is important to establish an educational institution and framework for overseas study that would foster the development of technocrats in charge of economic and financial matters with a high degree of integrity.

6

Speeding Up by Slowing Down: A Market-Building Approach to Financial Sector Reform

David C. Cole and Betty F. Slade

G IVEN THE MANY serious disruptions and financial crises that have been associated with recent attempts to modernize, privatize, and market-orient the financial systems in African countries, it would seem appropriate to consider some alternative approaches that focus on improving the basic components of the existing systems and moving toward the desired objectives over one or two decades rather than a few years. This paper outlines a more gradual, market-building approach to four major aspects of financial development: managing monetary policy; strengthening prudential regulation; improving financial services in rural areas; and promoting capital markets.

Managing Monetary Policy

Developing countries have recently been advised and encouraged to adopt market-based systems of monetary management—using open market operations with treasury bills or similar instruments to control the supply of reserve money, to influence interest rates, and to replace direct controls over credit allocation.[1] This market-based approach is

---

[1]See, for example, William E. Alexander, Tomás J.T. Baliño, and Charles Enoch, *The Adoption of Indirect Instruments of Monetary Policy,* IMF Occasional Paper No. 126 (Washington: International Monetary Fund, 1995).

seen as preferable to having monetary authorities set credit ceilings or guidelines, as well as interest rate ceilings and rate structures, that commonly fail to keep pace with changes in the rate of inflation or to reflect differences in credit quality or usage.

A number of countries have attempted to implement such market-based systems, but have encountered serious problems due to lack of fiscal discipline, absence of efficient, competitive markets for the new monetary instruments, and generally weak infrastructures of the financial system. Consequently, real interest rates have become unreasonably high or unstable, the monetary authorities have found it difficult to control key monetary variables, and, while some institutions and individuals have been hit hard, others have been able to exploit the new systems and markets to their own advantage.

Interest Rates and Exchange Rates

A transitional and less demanding alternative to trying to develop a "market-determined" level and structure of reference interest rates would be for the central bank to set fairly broad ranges for bank interest rates, and let individual banks set their own rates for different types of deposits and loans within the prescribed ranges. In the absence of a market-determined reference rate, the best available guide for interest rates is likely to be the recent rate of inflation, as measured by a consumer price index. The range for allowable bank deposit rates could be, for example, 0–10 percentage points above the national inflation rate of the most recent 3–6 months. A similar range of allowable bank loan rates should be prescribed, somewhat above the range for deposit rates, to allow for intermediation spreads (e.g., 5–20 percentage points above the inflation rate of recent months). Permitting banks to set their own rates for deposits and loans would give the banks an incentive to analyze their markets and costs of operations and to begin to explore strategies for increasing their profitability, important steps in preparing them for more market-based operations.

Similarly, instead of having a market-determined exchange rate, the central bank could adopt a crawling peg exchange rate linked to the differential rates of inflation of the home country and its main trading partners over the past 6–12 months. The central bank could set bands around the central rate at which it would be prepared to buy or sell foreign exchange. The central bank could widen the bands over time to allow more room for the foreign exchange market participants to trade with each other and to determine the daily rate within the bands.

Supply of Reserve Money

Rather than attempting a rapid transition from reliance on direct credit controls to use of open market operations for monetary management, the central bank could rely on the methods used in most developed countries over many decades—that is, control of the supply of reserve or base money and setting of legal reserve requirements as the primary constraint on total banking system credit and monetary expansion. A new approach to legal reserve requirements that distinguishes among the solvency, liquidity, and clearing roles of such reserves is outlined below in the discussion of prudential regulation.

For reserve money management, instead of open market operations or treasury bill auctions, the central bank could use much simpler instruments that have a direct impact on the supply of legal reserves and do not require elaborate new market instruments and mechanisms. For example, the central bank could participate directly in the interbank market, if one exists, by borrowing reserves from, or lending reserves to, individual banks at approximately the going interbank rates. It should avoid being a continuous borrower or a continuous lender of reserve funds in the interbank market because this would discourage development of trading between banks. Instead it should generally enter the market in an active way when it wishes to influence the level of reserve money and put some pressure on liquidity and interest rates. If an active interbank market does not exist, the central bank may be able to help get one started by offering to borrow or lend short-term funds from and to banks.

Through such participation in the interbank market, the central bank would not only be able to monitor directly the liquidity position of the banking system and of individual banks but also would be aware of pressures on the interbank interest rates. Utilization of the interbank market to manage the supply of reserve money, if done properly, would help to develop that market and provide an alternative to premature attempts to introduce bill auctions and the complex mechanisms required for trading such paper.

The central bank could also have authority to transfer deposits of government, or some government agencies, between the commercial banks and the central bank as a means of controlling the supply of reserve money. Such transfers could be done on a daily basis and distributed across the whole banking system in some equitable manner (as is the practice in Canada), or they could be done only on certain occasions when the other interbank and foreign exchange market instruments were not sufficient to achieve the needed adjustments in the supply of reserve money. Transfers of government deposits or leaving government deposits in individual banks should not, however, be used as a mechanism for subsidizing or penalizing individual banks.

The central bank should also have a rediscount window for banks that, for various reasons, could not be accommodated through the interbank market. For short-term borrowings the rediscount rate should be somewhat above the interbank rate, but it should rise steeply for longer-term users to discourage such demands.

The central bank could, and should, also participate directly in the foreign exchange market, as a buyer and seller at its own initiative and within the bands, in an effort to influence both the supply of reserves of the banking system and the exchange rate.

This approach to monetary management is designed to move the banking system in the direction of more market-oriented operations in gradual steps rather than quickly. It would provide room for increased bank discretion over both interest rates and sources and uses of funds, but within limits that were controlled by the monetary authorities. It would also give the central bank instruments for controlling the supply of reserve money that were not dependent on fully functioning money and capital markets. At the same time, it would open the way for developing money markets—including foreign exchange—which would subsequently facilitate use of indirect monetary policy instruments. Finally, it would give the banks more opportunity and experience in operating in such markets and eventually build the expertise to do so profitably and without excessive risk.

Strengthening Prudential Regulation

Elimination of interest rate and credit controls, especially if accompanied by either implicit or explicit government guarantees of bank liabilities and weak prudential supervision, has contributed to institutional failures and systemic crises in both developed and developing countries in recent years. A number of responses have been tried or proposed for resolving these problems, including strengthening prudential supervision, limiting the range of liabilities covered by deposit insurance or other government guarantees, limiting the kinds of assets that banks can hold to relatively low-risk instruments, and increasing required bank capital and linking it to the riskiness of the bank's assets. All of these suggestions have potential advantages, but they also have limitations and generally are very difficult to implement and enforce, especially in less-developed financial markets.[2]

---

[2]See, for example, Gerard Caprio, Jr., "Bank Regulation: The Case of the Missing Model," in *Sequencing? Financial Strategies for Developing Countries,* ed. by Alison Harwood and Bruce L.R. Smith (Washington: Brookings Institution, 1997), pp. 109–26.

There appears to be general agreement that prudential supervision of banks should be based upon active monitoring of the assets and the capital of individual banks by the central bank, or other designated agency, and that the regulatory system should be designed to provide incentives for prudential behavior by bank owners, managers, and regulators. The primary instrument for achieving this in many countries is the minimum required ratio of capital to risk-weighted assets. The more advanced countries have been working almost continuously to improve the original guidelines contained in the Basle Capital Accord of July 1988 so that the guidelines can better fit the requirements of today's increasingly complex financial markets.[3] However, the fundamental and very serious problem for many developing countries is not more sophisticated rules, but rather their very limited capability for supervising financial institutions and the related deficiencies in financial infrastructure (e.g., accounting, legal, and communications systems).

In developing countries, it is very difficult to monitor the quality of a bank's assets. It is also difficult to be sure that a bank has any real capital or even to be sure that it has liquid reserves to meet a sudden withdrawal of deposits. When a bank starts running into difficulty, the bank managers often attempt to hide the problems not just from the regulators but also from the depositors, and often even from the owners. The first sign of problems that the regulators are likely to see is when the bank is unable to meet its daily clearing obligations. When that happens, it usually means that the bank has already exhausted its liquid reserves and probably much of its capital.

One way to try to prevent this kind of liquidity and solvency crisis is to recast the traditional legal reserve requirement into three components that are specifically designed to meet the three separable objectives: solvency, liquidity, and clearing of daily settlements.

• Solvency is a medium- to long-run requirement for capital, or net worth, sufficient to meet all liabilities after liquidating assets.

• Liquidity is a short-run requirement for liquid assets that can be sold or pledged to obtain cash to meet temporary, adverse withdrawals of funds.

• Clearing balances are the normal working balances held at the central bank to meet daily settlements in the clearinghouse.

A powerful way to reinforce both the capital and liquidity requirements for banks would be to require banks to hold a *solvency reserve* and a *liquidity reserve* at the central bank. The solvency reserve should be linked to the bank's capital, while the liquidity reserve should be linked

---

[3]See the "Proposal to Issue a Supplement to the Basle Capital Accord to Cover Market Risks," issued by the Basle Committee on Banking Supervision, Basle, April 1995.

to the bank's deposit liabilities. The solvency reserve requirement might be equal to 50 percent of the bank's capital. The liquidity reserve requirement might be 10 percent of total deposit liabilities. Both reserve accounts could consist of domestic and/or foreign government securities that would be held by the central bank on behalf of the individual bank, which would receive the interest income derived from the securities. Both the solvency and liquidity reserves would be totally separate and distinct from a bank's required (clearing) reserve deposits at the central bank.

The *solvency reserve* would only be available for use by the central bank to help meet the obligations of the depositing bank in the event of closure and liquidation, or as part of a merger or acquisition of the bank. Holding the solvency reserve at the central bank would not prevent a bank from becoming insolvent, but it would at least give the central bank some good assets to help offset that insolvency. One objective of supervision would be to try to prevent a bank from reaching a level of insolvency such that the solvency reserve would not be able to meet the claims of creditors and depositors if liquidation became necessary. The required solvency reserve for individual banks could even be increased if, upon examination, it appeared that the bank was getting into difficulty. An increase in the required solvency reserve ratio would force a bank to transfer some securities from its liquidity reserve to its solvency reserve and then make adjustments in its assets and liabilities to bring its liquidity reserve back up to the required level.

The solvency reserve system is an alternative to, but very different from, deposit insurance. The main difference is that the solvency reserve is linked to the individual bank and is a partial guarantee of that bank's liabilities to its creditors. It is not a payment into a fund that serves to guarantee the claims of depositors at all participating banks, as insurance does.

After the end of each year, banks would be required to adjust their solvency reserve at the central bank to maintain the specified ratio. The central bank could withhold interest payments on the deposited securities if necessary to bring the reserve up to the required level.

The *liquidity reserve* is intended to meet extraordinary liquidity needs of a bank. Normal liquidity needs should be met out of other liquid assets that are held for such purposes and are not part of the formal liquidity reserve.

Each bank should be required to maintain the required balance in the liquidity reserve on average over a period of perhaps one month. It should be permitted to draw out up to perhaps 50 percent of the liquidity reserve for short periods of up to 15 days, but failure to bring the liquidity reserve account back up to the required level within that period or to maintain the average monthly requirement should be subject to severe penalties, including withholding of interest earnings on the securities in the account. Drawing the liquidity reserve down below 50 percent of the required level should require prior discussion with, and approval by, the central bank.

The *clearing reserve* is the clearing balance that banks need to maintain at the central bank to meet their clearing obligations at the end of the day. For purposes of uniformity, it may be desirable to set a *minimum required clearing reserve* of perhaps 2 percent of all third-party liabilities. Banks should be required to maintain this minimum on average over a two-week period. They should be subject to penalties if the average falls below the minimum. They should also be prohibited from having a negative clearing reserve at the end of any day. It would be much easier to have accurate information on each bank's clearing reserve position if such reserves were defined as deposits at the central bank and did not include vault cash or any other items.

Introduction of the solvency and liquidity reserve requirements could be facilitated for existing banks by a concurrent reduction in the current legal reserve requirement that would free up an approximately equivalent amount of reserve deposits that could be transferred to the solvency and liquidity reserve accounts. Most developing countries have relatively high required reserve ratios. A reduction in these ratios would be warranted in its own right to reduce the amount of nonearning assets of the banks. Transferring the funds to the solvency and liquidity reserve accounts would turn them into earning assets, but it would not result in any immediate change in the liquidity of the banking system that might call for neutralizing action by the central bank. Once the initial adjustment had been made, banks would henceforth be required to maintain their several reserve deposit accounts on a continuing basis.

New banks should be required to meet the established solvency, liquidity, and clearing reserve ratios from the inception of their operations. Initially the solvency reserve would account for a relatively large portion of the new bank's total assets, but as third-party liabilities and other earning assets grew, the solvency reserve would diminish in relative importance until it stabilized at about 5–6 percent of the bank's total assets. The solvency reserve might be increased for individual banks to 10 percent or even 20 percent of total assets if those banks were perceived to be heading for insolvency. The liquidity and clearing reserve deposits, on the other hand, would initially be a small share of total assets but would then rise, as third-party liabilities grew, to become a relatively constant share of total assets commensurate with the required reserve ratios.

The suggested system of solvency and liquidity reserves is not a substitute for bank supervision, but rather an attempt to reinforce effective supervision and at the same time to provide an alternative to deposit insurance that is less susceptible to moral hazard and exploitation by unscrupulous bank owners and managers. Such reserve requirements should help to open the way for less restricted entry of new banks and expansion of existing banks that might be expected to occur with the removal of direct controls over banking activities. If some banks, especially state-owned banks, could not be expected to conform to the new decontrolled system, they should be excluded from the privileges and requirements of that system and treated as special cases.

Improving Financial Services in Rural Areas

The financial services that urban-based officials tend to believe are most needed in rural areas are production credits and means of making payments between rural and urban areas. The experience of many developing countries that have viable rural financial institutions, both formal and informal, is that the main need is for a secure form of savings and, secondarily, for short-term consumption credits. Payment services are more often needed by larger traders and by urban residents who wish to transfer funds to their relatives in the rural areas. Production credits are often part of government-sponsored programs and have generally been shown to be unnecessary to gain acceptance of "good" programs. Moreover, they are likely to benefit the better-off rural inhabitants and those who manage the programs, rather than the rural poor.

The primary focus of rural financial service improvement programs should, therefore, be on improving savings facilities. This entails making such services convenient, accessible, and safe. Whether such savings facilities should be provided by an entity that also extends credit is a difficult issue. It is the extension of credit that generally leads to nonperforming loans and inability to reimburse depositors. If safety, convenience, and liquidity of deposits are the primary objective, then only those deposit-mobilizing institutions that have a viable capability for administering loan programs effectively should be permitted to use the depositors' funds to make such loans. Otherwise the funds should be invested in other ways that would assure safety and a reasonable return. A central bank that wished to promote such deposit-mobilizing institutions could even consider accepting deposits from those institutions and paying them a positive real rate of interest.

The postal service is an entity that might be encouraged to concentrate on deposit mobilization. Unfortunately, in some countries that have postal savings banks, those institutions are attempting to become lending institutions serving the needs of small borrowers. This is more than likely to lead to nonperforming loans, insolvency, and a call upon the central bank for a bailout. The alternative of concentrating on deposit mobilization and lending the proceeds to the central bank or to sound commercial banks at a viable interbank rate should be considered.

Promoting Capital Markets

The experience in most Asian developing countries has been that capital markets began to play a significant role only after the banking system was reasonably well developed. Capital markets are not a substitute for an inefficient banking system, as Popiel has suggested,[4] but, in fact, require the services of an efficient banking system to be able to function efficiently themselves. Therefore, in the early stages of financial development the focus should be on the banking system and creating an environment in which it can grow and provide the many services for which it is intended and generally best suited.

As a rough rule of thumb, based on Asian experience, it is probably unrealistic to expect capital markets to play a significant role in mobilizing and allocating savings in a country until the ratio of M2 to GDP has reached at least 40 percent, and the ratio of M2 to M1 is in the range of 3 or 4 to 1. Such ratios tend to indicate that the banking system has managed to become a significant mobilizer of financial savings, which also suggests that inflation is not a major problem and that the public has some confidence in the safety and soundness of the banking institutions, as well as the monetary and fiscal policies of the government. It also is likely to indicate that money markets, especially the interbank markets, are already functioning.

Capital markets have two important "hidden" costs that are not widely appreciated. The first is that stock market indexes, no matter how small or inefficient the market, often become "barometers" of overall economic performance that can affect capital flows, international borrowing costs, and even the tenure of senior government officials. As a consequence, there is a strong temptation for governments to promote rises in the index, and to resort to various nonmarket measures to prevent excessive declines.

---

[4]Paul A. Popiel, *Financial Systems in Sub-Saharan Africa: A Comparative Study,* World Bank Discussion Paper, Africa Technical Department Series, No. 260 (Washington: World Bank, 1994).

The second hidden cost is the time of both senior government officials and financial specialists in government agencies and private institutions that are expended on setting up capital market institutions, attempting to provide adequate regulation, and dealing with the problems and crises that inevitably arise. These costs are in addition to the more obvious real resources that go into building the stock exchanges, trading and clearing systems, and communication facilities that efficient capital markets require, as well as the often highly trained human resources that are directly involved in operating the capital market institutions. All these costs need to be weighed against the positive benefits that may be derivable from the capital markets in assessing when it is justifiable for individual countries to begin promoting their development.[5]

Conclusion

Current efforts to transform quickly the financial systems of developing countries from directly controlled, often insolvent institutions to healthy, market-oriented, and indirectly regulated institutions are encountering serious problems. Efficient financial markets, well-managed financial institutions, reliable information and communication systems, competent monetary policy managers, and prudential regulators cannot be created in a brief period, especially in countries with unstable political systems, and limited human capital and physical infrastructure.

The alternative is to follow an evolutionary strategy that seeks to address the most serious problems sequentially with measures and instruments that not only are practical within the existing constraints but also will help to open the way for further refinements in the future. This paper has suggested approaches to managing monetary policy (including determining interest rates and exchange rates, setting reserve requirements, and managing reserve money), strengthening prudential

---

[5]Professor Kapur, in commenting on this paper, suggested that Yoon Je Cho, in his "Inefficiencies from Financial Liberalization in the Absence of Well-Functioning Equity Markets," *Journal of Money, Credit and Banking,* Vol. 18 (May 1986), had developed a strong theoretical argument for the early introduction of equity markets in order to achieve more efficient allocation of capital and risk sharing in a liberalized financial environment. As we read Cho's argument, he is really making a case for venture capital companies to mobilize funds from limited numbers of high-risk, high-return investors and channel such funds into matching types of enterprises. We would agree that this could be a useful form of intermediation in some countries, and that equity markets may eventually play a role in distributing shares of successful venture capital investments. But they are not necessary to the process and, if introduced prematurely, their costs may more than offset any benefits deriving from this role.

regulation of banks, improving rural financial services (especially savings facilities), and developing money and capital markets that are consistent with this kind of evolutionary strategy for financial restructuring in countries in the early stages of financial development.

Comments

Basant Kapur

I think both of the papers on financial sector reform are very thought-provoking, but I propose to confine my comments to the paper by David Cole and Betty Slade since my own past research has focused on the problems of the less-developed countries rather than on the somewhat different problems of the formerly socialist economies. Cole and Slade advocate an evolutionary approach to financial sector reform based on their recognition that many developing countries, particularly in Africa, do not currently have in place full-fledged market-based financial systems.

My comments will be organized around four broad themes, which follow the order of the Cole and Slade paper. First, on monetary policy management, Cole and Slade recommend that the central bank allow bank deposit rates to be set by individual banks within a range of, "for example, 0–10 percentage points above the national inflation rate of the most recent 3–6 months." The range for allowable bank loan rates could correspondingly be, for example, 5–20 percentage points above the recent inflation rate. Similarly, they propose "a crawling peg exchange rate linked to the differential rates of inflation of the home country and its main trading partners over the past 6–12 months," with bands around the central rate. They also advocate central bank participation in the interbank and foreign exchange markets and the opening of a rediscount window.

One missing feature in these proposals is any reference to a nominal anchor for the system. Unanticipated shocks to money demand or supply, for example, could lead to short-run variations in the domestic inflation rate, which would then be "validated" by automatic adjustments of the rate of crawl of the exchange rate. So there may be a problem of indeterminacy of the equilibrium price level.

Another missing feature is any reference to the relationship between interest rates and the rate of change of the exchange rate. The greater the degree of financial capital mobility enjoyed by the country, the less domestic interest rates can be set independently of the rate of crawl of the exchange rate without triggering potentially destabilizing capital inflows or outflows.

If capital mobility is imperfect, there is greater scope for domestic variations in interest rates, but it must then be recognized that interest rates are an important control instrument. They have to be carefully manipulated to achieve an efficient time path of disinflation of highly inflationary economies, and in this process, too, they have to be coordinated with the trajectory of exchange rate changes. Once disinflation is achieved, interest rates have to be kept at reasonable positive levels in real terms and must, as earlier mentioned, be monitored to ensure that they do not get too much out of synchronization with the exchange rate crawl.

My own preference would be, therefore, to organize the discussion of monetary policy management around a target rate of disinflation and around maintenance of a low steady-state inflation rate. The Asian experience has shown that sustained low inflation rates in the neighborhood of about 3–10 percent a year are conducive to sustained economic growth. Central bank management of the monetary base and the exchange rate, as well as the fiscal policy stance, should, in my view, be geared to this primary objective. Once a low steady-state rate of inflation is achieved, commercial banks could be given leeway to set deposit and lending rates, perhaps within bands, as suggested by Cole and Slade, but prior to that the central bank may need to more actively manipulate interest rates, along with the exchange rate, in the process of implementing an efficient stabilization and disinflation strategy. Failure to do so could well result in erratic swings in deposit and lending rates that would interfere with an orderly stabilization program.

Second, on the issue of prudential management of banks and Cole and Slade's proposed new approach to reserve requirements, the novel feature here is their proposal for the establishment of a solvency reserve requirement that could be 50 percent of the bank's capital. Such a reserve would presumably serve two main functions: first, as suggested, it could be used by the central bank to help meet the obligations of a defaulting bank; and, second, the prospect of its forfeiture in the event of default would increase the cost of default to the bank's owners and thus strengthen their incentive to refrain from actions that increase the likelihood of default.

I must confess to being somewhat dubious about the efficacy of the solvency requirement. As Cole and Slade point out, the solvency requirement would amount to only 5–6 percent of the total assets of an established bank that had large third-party, including deposit, liabilities. It is not clear that such a small percentage provides much of a disincentive to misuse of the bank's assets by its owners and managers for their own benefit, should they be so inclined.

For new banks, the solvency requirement would weigh much more heavily, but it is not clear, especially if they were domestic banks, that they could afford to have such a large proportion of their capital immobilized in the vault of the central bank and unavailable for productive deployment. The danger then is that the establishment of potentially viable new domestic banks would be discouraged in favor of existing banks and foreign banks with access to much larger capital resources.

My view, therefore, is that there really is no substitute for the slow, hard route of improving the transparency and accountability of the financial system. As the authors point out, this requires vastly improved accounting, legal, and communications systems and a strengthened regulatory and supervisory framework. Since we are dealing here with issues of values and ethics as well, it also requires that attention be paid to strengthening the corporate culture of banks, especially in terms of the moral stance and outlook of bank owners and managers, and this in turn may require linking the corporate culture to the values and ideology of the society at large. Here I must indicate my strong agreement with the thrust of Tetsuji Tanaka's concluding paragraph. In addition, case studies of successful banks in the developing world could provide valuable insights and inspiration.

On a somewhat different issue, the regulatory and supervisory improvements may also need to deal with the issue of market structure and competition policy, particularly when, as is often the case, the banking system is oligopolistic or cartelized.

Third, Cole and Slade discuss the issue of financial services in rural areas. While provision of convenient and safe deposit facilities is undoubtedly very important, I cannot agree with the authors that the provision of production credits is of secondary importance. This is particularly true in regard to the provision of production credits to the rural poor. Formal financial institutions have been notably unsuccessful in meeting the credit needs of the rural poor, owing to the high transactions costs, broadly defined, relative to the size of the loans that are entailed.

Over the past decade or so, however, great progress has been achieved by so-called community-based lending programs in meeting this need. The most prominent example is, of course, that of the Grameen Bank in Bangladesh, but there are other examples as well: in Asia, the Badan Kredit Kecamatan and the Bank Rakyat Indonesian Unit Desas in Indonesia, and the Bank of Agriculture and Agricultural Cooperatives in Thailand; in Africa, a joint liability program in Zimbabwe, the Credit Solidaire in Burkina Faso, and the Smallholder Agricultural Credit Administration in Malawi.

The distinctive feature of all these institutions is that the community is brought into the process of screening loan applicants or in helping to ensure loan repayments. For example, in the case of the Grameen Bank, borrowers are asked to form credit groups, and if one member of a group defaults, the whole group is liable for the defaulting member's repayment. There is, thus, strong social pressure on members of these self-formed groups not to default.

In the case of the Indonesian institutions, local officials, community leaders, and village heads are brought into the borrower selection process, and, again, there is social pressure on the borrowers who have been so selected not to default. Experience with these community-based lending programs has to date been generally highly positive. Positive real lending rates have been sustained, outreach has grown substantially, and the rates of loan repayment have been high. Transaction costs are low and the rural poor are able to obtain small sums of credit, which are, nevertheless, very helpful in enabling them to upgrade their productive activities. There appears to be considerable scope, therefore, for a vastly enlarged role for such programs in less-developed countries.

Fourth, and last, on the promotion of capital markets, Cole and Slade argue that this should be done after the banking system is reasonably well developed. There is merit to this point of view, although a countervailing argument is provided in the well-known paper by Yoon Je Cho, "Inefficiencies from Financial Liberalization in the Absence of Well-Functioning Equity Markets," published in the *Journal of Money, Credit and Banking* in May 1986. Essentially, Cho argues that the fixed-fee nature of debt contracts, coupled with asymmetric information between sources and users of funds, could well result in the banking system passing up investment projects that are perceived by it to be risky but that should, on a social cost-benefit calculus, be taken up. However, equity finance would not be subject to this limitation, as it is not based on fixed-fee contracts. Cho also recognizes that full-fledged equity markets may take time to develop, and he suggests allowing banks to take equity positions in the corporate sector (i.e., universal banking), although he recognizes that this, too, may create problems.

A possible compromise would be to allow banks to set up venture capital funds, either on their own or jointly with other sources of finance. This would not require the banks to convert themselves wholesale into universal banks, but it would help to ensure a supply of valuable equity finance for potentially worthwhile projects, even before fully developed equity markets are in place.

As a brief summing up, I would like to say that I am sympathetic to Cole and Slade's position that the transition to a market-based system of monetary management, involving open-market operations in treasury bills or similar instruments, may take time. However, I believe that even accepting this as a short-run constraint, more can be done than their paper seems to suggest, and my comments have essentially been aimed at filling in what I consider some of the main gaps in their discussion.

Patrick Downes

Listening to David Cole's caution about rushing headlong into market-based systems of monetary management brought to my mind the views that Keynes had about the type of people that should run the IMF—he said that they should be cautious bankers. I had the feeling that we were failing him [Keynes] seriously until Basant Kapur came to our rescue a little bit by emphasizing that financial reforms have to be coherent and grounded in macrostabilization programs. But I should mention in passing that Keynes also had the view that the Board of the World Bank should be imaginative expansionists! I hope we are neither cautious bankers nor imaginative expansionists.

The Kyrgyz Republic

Before coming to the paper by David Cole and Betty Slade let me address Tetsuji Tanaka's paper. I have three main comments. First, the restructuring of the financial sector and the economy at large is a huge undertaking in any state of the former Soviet Union. The transformation in the Kyrgyz Republic started four or five years ago, and it is well under way. It requires major economic reforms in a host of related areas, including rebuilding economic and trading relations with other countries on a comparative advantage basis, and the legal, regulatory, and institutional framework to support these changes. Policies have to be formulated in conformity with the particular realities of that individual country, but given the wide scope of necessary reforms—and financial sector reforms have a significant influence on the success of the stabilization efforts—speed and depth are most important to ensure success in this process.

Second, the task of reform is far from over, and a price must be paid for the transformation. Tanaka makes that quite clear, although the shock therapy that he talks about in a sense was already administered when the existing system of economic, trade, and financial relations with other countries broke down. However, in the light of some recent economic developments and statistics, I am somewhat more optimistic about prospects in the Kyrgyz Republic than Tanaka. While industrial output continued to decline in 1995, agricultural production rebounded following the dismantling of the state agricultural production system. The services and trade sectors have also expanded rapidly with the liberalization of the trade and exchange system; the authorities estimate that the emerging private sector not yet covered in official statistics already amounts to 10–20 percent of GDP. In terms of the success that the Kyrgyz Republic has had in controlling inflation, I think it has now joined the group of countries that have succeeded in getting inflation down to 20–30 percent a year. Interest rates, of course, are positive in real terms, and, as Tanaka has said, the currency, the som, has been pretty stable in recent times. Moreover, in 1995, for the first time in five years, GNP actually rose.

But I think the jury is still out. There is a lot of work to be done, and that brings me to the third point—the appropriate degree of government intervention in markets. This is unique in every country and is related, as Tanaka says, to the maturity of the markets. But it is clear that the government in the Kyrgyz Republic has a strong commitment to developing markets and appropriate regulatory institutions; we have to allow some time for these measures to take hold, and it is going to take time. The financial reform process is a continuous one, and it would be a waste of resources to develop market institutions and implement financial reforms and not adhere to them.

Finally, in the countries of the former Soviet Union, there is no shortage of voices calling for reinstitution of heavy state intervention in the economy. It seems, therefore, that a more activist stance is called for in championing the cause of free markets in countries like the Kyrgyz Republic, even more so perhaps than in Africa, where the historical experience has been quite different. Indeed, this championing of the cause of free markets is vital to ensure that the country remains on course. There are some very difficult decisions to be made, for example, in relation to restructuring the banking system and the enterprise sector.

What lessons can we draw from the experience of the Kyrgyz Republic? Tanaka refers to the work and business ethic, and that is clearly very important. Another lesson perhaps that may have some relevance for African countries is the sense in which the financial sector reforms were grounded in a macroeconomic stabilization program, and I think that clearly establishes the interlinkages, or the symbiosis, between financial sector reform and other structural reforms and progress toward stabilization. Kapur has flagged this also in his comments on the Cole and Slade paper.

The Speed of Reform

Moving to the Cole and Slade paper, it is an interesting paper, nicely crafted and thoughtful in many respects, and designed, I think, to challenge the conventional thinking about financial sector reform. As the paper is intended to be general, it cannot be expected to apply fully to the broad variety of situations in African countries; indeed, many have recorded solid progress with financial reforms in recent times. It quite rightly calls attention to the fact that financial reforms sometimes fail, at least temporarily, because the authorities attempt to go too fast or because some of the concomitant reforms are not present, such as fiscal consolidation and effective banking supervision capability.

But I believe that Cole and Slade do not quite accurately describe the current market-based "orthodoxy," if we can call it that—especially when they refer to the IMF Occasional Paper by Alexander and others on adoption of indirect monetary instruments.[1] Indeed, what the paper advocates is a gradual—"belt and braces," if necessary—approach to the adoption of indirect instruments and financial reform in general, but we are convinced that the market-based system is the right way to go. Of course, there are prior or concomitant reforms that need to be addressed (e.g., fiscal discipline, a sound and competitive banking system and a proper regulatory framework, insulation of monetary policy from deficit financing, and promotion of money markets and primary and secondary government securities markets).

So we do advocate a cautious approach on financial reforms, but caution should not be interpreted in the sense of being a delayed approach. Our view is that financial reform measures should be taken as soon as they can be taken, and I think this captures something that Kwesi Botchwey said this morning as well—that is, the importance of spelling out these structural measures in the context of an overall macroeconomic approach to stabilization.

Turning to the actual measures that have been suggested in the Cole and Slade paper, I agree very much with Kapur's comments, so I will touch only on a few issues. On the proposal for a crawling peg system within a band, I doubt such an exchange rate system can be prescribed for all African countries—it has to be very much a case-by-case approach—and I would emphasize the importance of coordinating interest and exchange rate policies.

Then there is the proposal on solvency and liquidity, which purports to be a substitute in a sense for a more conventional system of banking supervision. I quite agree that the banking supervision norms of the Group of Ten countries are not necessarily a good fit for developing countries in Africa. There is a need to develop guidelines that could draw on the best practices in developed countries but that are adjusted to the conditions in developing countries where risk is often higher. The IMF and the World Bank have done some work in this area in the last few years, and there is a need for follow-up. But I doubt that the

---

[1]William E. Alexander, Tomás J.T. Baliño, and Charles Enoch, *The Adoption of Indirect Instruments of Monetary Policy*, IMF Occasional Paper No. 126 (Washington: International Monetary Fund, 1995).

arrangement proposed in the Cole and Slade paper can substitute for a prudentially based banking supervision framework.

Coming to the proposal for a band—a floor and ceiling—on interest rates, this is nothing new in financial reform. It has been an intermediate stage of financial reform that has been in vogue for a number of years, and it is a good idea. But there is always a danger: when one is stipulating floors and ceilings, one is still close to administering rates— or at least on a slippery slope in that direction—and competition and resource allocation distortions can ensue. There may, of course, be cause to delay interest rate liberalization if bank supervision is inadequate, but I would be skeptical of any suggestion to impose controls on a system that has already been liberalized.

On controlling the supply of reserve money, the paper has some interesting ideas but, again, I felt what was missing—and Kapur put his finger on it quite clearly—was how this fits into both a macroeconomic framework and an anti-inflation stabilization program with a suitable nominal anchor. There seems to be no mention in the paper of how fiscal deficits of the government are going to be dealt with. Burgeoning fiscal deficits have been responsible for derailing many financial reform programs, certainly as much as, if not more so than, soundness problems in the banking system.

I have the feeling that quite a number of the measures that are being suggested—and Kapur has dealt with these—seem to put financial reforms in a type of holding pattern, leaving the underlying distortions possibly not addressed. In that case, the distortions most likely will become chronic and the ultimate cost—most frequently to the public purse—of, for example, sorting out problems in the bank portfolios will increase. Competition only works if there is a willingness to allow problem enterprises and banks to fail. Indeed, I think a number of African countries have postponed implementing solutions to banking soundness problems, only to see the problems grow.

On managing reserve money, several of the instruments that have been suggested—that is, the central bank getting involved in the interbank market and moving government deposits to banks to influence the reserves—raise concerns in my mind about the credit risk aspects of these arrangements as there is a danger of moral hazard. I would rather see a central bank promoting, but not participating in, the development of an active interbank market.

But overall my concerns are with what is missing in the framework— that is, the coordination of monetary and fiscal policies, a marriage that must exist in developing countries as they progress to develop financial markets. The government has to borrow money, and encouraging the government to borrow at a market rate and in the marketplace seems a more sensible way to proceed than what has happened in many countries—the government borrowing directly from the central bank at low or no interest rates and engaging in monetary financing and obliging banks to take up low-interest government debt, very often crowding out the private sector. Indeed, I think one of the most serious problems in a number of African countries has been excessive borrowing by governments from central banks with inflationary consequences and building up huge quasi-fiscal losses that have not been addressed. Finally, I do not see how the measures proposed would protect the system from catastrophe, at least any more so than the more direct approach of relying on market-based interest rates and exchange rates, and developing financial markets.

Let me sum up. I concur with Kapur on his approach to a lot of the issues raised in the Cole and Slade paper. Certainly, it is appealing to think in terms of a cautious approach to financial sector reform in African countries and, as one participant here remarked, to remember that it took Japan 50–100 years. But I wonder if African countries can afford to wait that long. With economic globalization and the integration of financial markets, there is a danger that countries in Africa, the poorer countries, may be marginalized and left behind—all the more so as official aid flows start to dry up and the large private capital flows increasingly gravitate to emerging market countries. So there is a battle to be joined here, a task to be addressed. I think the problems of unsound banking systems and misallocation of resources, whether through directed credits, subsidized credit, unrepresentative interest rates, or excessive government borrowing from the central bank, must be brought out into the open and dealt with in a transparent fashion. And adopting—gradually if necessary—financial liberalization and reforms and a market-based approach to monetary management using indirect instruments is the best way to go. If problems occur when financial reforms go off the rail, especially as a result of fiscal profligacy, it is important that the costs are clear and transparent so that they can be addressed.

Tadahiko Nakagawa

I would like to commend the two speakers. In particular, I fully agree with Tetsuji Tanaka's remark that the financial sector is one of the most important social infrastructures and that appropriate government intervention in the financial sector, including by the central bank, is crucial. I also share the view expressed by David Cole when he spoke about the need for a gradual approach to financial reforms in African countries.

Let me briefly present the experiences of the Export-Import Bank of Japan (JEXIM) with client governments in assisting financial sector reform. My comment is basically focused on the area of long-term financing because the scope of financial sector reform is so vast and it is very difficult for me to elaborate in depth on all of the areas.

I would like to examine our financial assistance in Tunisia and Hungary. Although these cases are not simply or automatically applicable to the countries you represent here around this table, I think we could find some common ground to explore in the future for attaining financial reform.

Two-Step Loans in Tunisia

In the case of Tunisia, we have tried to support financial sector reform with structural adjustment loans, cofinanced with the World Bank. At the same time, we have lent money to the Tunisian Development Bank in the form of so-called two-step loans—JEXIM lends the money to a bank (or banks) in a particular country, and then the bank onlends the money to individual enterprises. This type of loan, or "onlending," is aimed at supporting the investment activities of mainly small and medium-sized private firms (preferably in priority exporting sectors). It fills a vacuum, in that countries in an early stage of development lack both a capital market and the necessary long-term financing for investment.

Back in March of 1996, we visited Tunisia to appraise our first and second two-step loans. We found that through loans of approximately $170 million ($70 million committed in 1989 and $100 million in 1993), we were able to support more than 100 projects—helping to create 10,000 jobs (mainly in tourism and manufacturing)—for a value added of about $200 million.

Even more impressive was the strong institutional building that had taken place in the client bank since 1989. The bank has a very fine team of credit analysts and risk management personnel, and I was delighted to learn that they had introduced a preliminary Asset Liability Management System—a system that is not even quite completed in our own bank. I was impressed by the talented team that explained specific kinds of projects to us, virtually every one of which has been a success.

Thanks to this preliminary postoperation evaluation study, we have determined that although a market approach serves as a sound basis for financial reform, some types of creative interventions and controls—in this case, our two-step loans—can help support or complement the market system.

Two-Step Loans in Hungary

In the case of Hungary, we started a similar two-step loan in 1992 and conducted a relatively comprehensive postoperation evaluation in 1995. The loan was for approximately $130 million, ultimately supporting 1,000 projects through ten banks—roughly half of which were very traditional banks (formerly government-owned banks), with the remaining foreign owned. Thus, in Hungary, as in Tunisia, we felt that our two-step loans really helped pave the way for future financial reform in a country at a transitional stage of development.

In Hungary, one of the most difficult questions has been determining the appropriate margin for the intermediary banks—that is, the fee paid to the banks that do the onlending to the private sector. This is still an unsolved problem. Some of the Hungarian banks (basically foreign-owned ones) are quite satisfied with the 2 percent margin that was fixed at the time, because they are dealing with established multinational corporations. However, other banks (basically, existing local Hungarian banks with an enormously high cost structure) would like wider margins so that they can lend to so-called new entrepreneurs—who are vitally important for the future of the country but are not perfectly creditworthy and lack sufficient collateral.

We think that the question of margins will be one of the central issues in our future discussions. For a country such as Hungary, which has an enormous shortage of long-term financial resources, it might be worthwhile for the intermediary banks to assume a certain amount of risk (managed risk) with a wider margin. Indeed, we might support this type of initiative in the future.

Conclusions

Based on these two transactions, we can conclude that the financial sector is critical for the development of private enterprise. Moreover, securing long-term financing is the key to supporting the fixed direct investments of those companies that are, in turn, critical for economic growth. And what is important is some kind of market-friendly intervention—in these cases, our two-step loans—at a transitional stage of financial reform in a country.

Although we have not yet tried these types of transactions in the sub-Saharan African countries, we are contemplating doing so, if it is feasible and reasonable.

General Discussion

Accelerating Fiscal and Financial Sector Reforms

In reaction to Peter Heller's comment that countries should try to reduce their reliance on export taxation, *Jean-Claude Brou* of Côte d'Ivoire suggested that the problem was one of timing, and not whether such a step should be taken at all. If countries reduced those taxes too rapidly, trying to replace them with taxes on domestic consumption, a problem would arise because most African economies were rural and agricultural in nature, and the informal sector was still a substantial sector. Moreover, increasing taxes on domestic consumption required a strong fiscal administration—which took time to create—whereas reducing taxes on international trade could have an immediate impact on revenues. Thus, it needed to be recognized that the substitution process would take time, and if things were done too quickly, other imbalances would occur, in turn slowing down the entire readjustment process.

As for Heller's suggestion that countries reduce and control tax exemptions, Brou pointed out that countries often ran into difficulties trying to do that because most exemptions were linked to investment codes and most developing countries offered such exemptions. Côte d'Ivoire had introduced a new investment code in 1995 after concluding that it needed to maintain a certain level of exemptions just to remain competitive.

Kwesi Botchwey of Ghana concurred with Brou's and Heller's assessment of the problem, noting that Ghana had once or twice committed itself to removing exemptions but then ran into legal obstacles because the exemptions were embedded in investment codes or aid agreements that stipulated that none of the aid resources could be used to pay taxes (which tax officials interpreted to mean exemptions for everyone). In addition, a study by the minerals commission showed that Ghana's investment codes were quite competitive, and tampering with the codes would risk investor confidence. So in the end, Ghana had decided to leave the codes alone and focus on the problem of abuse. It had quickly clamped down on the extreme instances of tax exemptions for plant and equipment for mining being misused through the importation of luxury vehicles. But what could be done when the exemptions were embedded in legislation and countries had to position themselves competitively? Where was the leeway for countries concerned about effective duty rates?

Aliou Seck of Senegal concurred that governments needed to mobilize as much revenue as possible, something Senegal had been trying to do—in part by introducing a tax on the informal market and eliminating exemptions that were no longer needed. But he also stressed that external resources needed to be clearly programmed and arrive on time.

Soumaïla Cissé of Mali pointed out that his country had worked with the IMF on trying to improve the fiscal situation but had run into difficulties when donors opposed the reduction of taxes. What should countries do in such situations? As for strengthening tax administration, Cissé asked how Heller thought countries could do so while simultaneously spending more on education and health and yet limiting the number of wage earners and holding down salaries. There were only 52 cards in a deck, which the IMF wanted countries to reshuffle and deal out again. There were constraints everywhere, and countries had to rethink priorities.

The private sector perspective was introduced by *Edouard Luboya* of Zaïre, who observed that the seminar so far had focused strictly on the public sector, whereas it was the private sector that had made a significant contribution to Zaïre's recent progress in lowering inflation and generating revenue. The government was now including private sector representatives in certain monthly economic discussions at the central bank, and it was important that the private sector actively participate in the design and implementation of adjustment measures. Regarding mobilization of revenues, he remarked that although procedures needed to be put in place to improve tax collections, the state should motivate taxpayers by providing better and more visible services. And tax collection efforts needed to be equitable, not singling out certain companies.

Heller responded to concerns about exemptions by noting that, first, most studies of investment incentives, particularly by the World Bank, raised questions about whether countries really gained very much by having those kinds of tax incentives. Second, to the extent countries had those incentives, there should be a "sunset rule," perhaps ending the exemption after three or four years. Third, it was better to have those provisions in tax codes, so that policymakers could look at the tax codes in an integrated way. Fourth, competition was not a function of exemptions alone, but also of tax rates and other tax provisions—with many exemptions, tax rates would need to be higher, given the narrower tax base. In sum, the goal should be to limit these exemptions and lower the tax rate at the same time. Heller conceded that, to some extent, the room for maneuver was limited, because many donors insisted on certain types of exemptions for their projects. But the key was to at least avoid the extent to which such exemptions created the opportunities for abuse and the sort of unmandated expansion of eligibility for particular exemptions beyond what they were ever intended to be.

Turning to Brou's concern about the timing for elimination of export taxes and the raising of domestic consumption taxes, Heller pointed out that the tax base for domestic consumption—at least domestic consumption that could be taxed—was effectively limited to imports and to what was produced by domestic manufacturing enterprises. No one expected countries to tax agricultural goods produced by subsistence farmers for consumption. So by extending the tax beyond imports to domestic producers of the same good, at least the tax base could be broadened. Heller conceded that there were some cases where export taxes might be appropriate and relevant, such as when there was very limited domestic consumption of the exportable good, but those cases were extremely limited in number.

As for concerns about equity, Heller said the IMF was simply suggesting that countries focus their tax efforts on the larger enterprises above a certain scale—those that provide the government with 80–90 percent of the revenues—because that was much more efficient in an administrative sense. Otherwise, tremendous and limited administrative resources were wasted. Of course, it was important to have some way of covering the smaller enterprises, but they were already in the tax net to the extent that they had to pay taxes on imported inputs.

Heller sympathized with Cissé about the feeling that "there are only 52 cards in a deck," agreeing that it was hard to do everything at the same time. But he argued that a strong, well-run tax administration, run by well-paid tax administrators, paid for itself. It was a net gainer for the economy. That was one of the reasons why Uganda and several other countries had sought to move the tax administration out of the civil service and put it on a better paid autonomous basis.

Finally, Heller responded to Shahid Yusuf's observation that East Asia only began introducing significant fiscal reforms in the early to mid-1980s, and Africa was following with a decade's lag. Heller said he knew where Asia had been 20 years ago and where Africa was today, but sometimes he wished that Africa today were where it had been 20 years ago—in that case, most countries would be much better off. So the question was: How was Africa going to get from where it was now to where it wanted to be—rather than to continue to follow the path of the past 10 or 15 years, which had been one of major setbacks?

On the topic of financial reform, Botchwey agreed with David Cole that individual country circumstances might dictate the need to proceed cautiously, but for Ghana, at least, a quick move to a market-oriented exchange rate and interest rate system helped depersonalize and de-politicize decision making. Initially, Ghana had tried the gradual approach to exchange rate reform until policymakers decided it was impossible to proceed that way. Whenever the exchange rate needed to be adjusted, even the slightest bit, according to the agreed formula, it took long meetings in the middle of the night, with daggers drawn. Eventually, policymakers realized that the only way to end the paralysis was to adopt a market-based system overnight, and, interestingly, those who were the most vociferous in opposing even the smallest changes very quickly got used to what the market said and did. A similar dynamic occurred in the case of interest rates, with overnight reform alleviating the pressure on the central bank and commercial banks to influence the Minister of Finance.

George Anthony Chigora of Zimbabwe, however, emphasized the need for a more gradual, market-building approach, noting that the abrupt measures have tended to be abandoned by some countries. He went on to say that developing countries were being asked to change in a very short time what had taken other countries a very long time.

Cissé raised the issue of stability in policymaking, suggesting that countries such as Indonesia had found it easier to succeed with reforms because the Minister of Finance there, for example, had held his position for 20 years. If a country had the same ministers and advisors for a long period of time, there was a certain continuity. But for Africa the opposite had occurred, resulting in a lot of go, no-go, starts, and stops. As for the speed of reform, Cissé acknowledged that there was a need for patience. But he worried that given the changed economic environment—replete with Internet and cable television—Africa had to accelerate or risk being swept out of the way.

David Cole responded that he, too, desired rapid development of the financial system. But his main point was that if countries tried to go too fast and leap over some of the necessary developmental steps, the result would be a slowing down of the entire liberalization process. That did not necessarily mean, however, that countries had to follow the same sequences as others before them. A great deal could be learned from the use of modern communication systems.

How about Basant Kapur's concern—a concern also raised by Patrick Downes—that there was no reference to a nominal anchor in the Cole and Slade proposals, meaning that unanticipated shocks to money demand or supply, for example, could lead to short-run variations in the domestic inflation rate, which would then be "validated" by automatic adjustments of the rate of crawl of the exchange rate? Cole countered that a nominal anchor was not the real issue, but rather that there were other ways of trying to control reserve money besides treasury bill open-market operations. Reserve money growth could be a target or nominal anchor, as could the inflation rate of nominal GDP. It was important, however, that this not be implemented in a rigid way. Flexibility of both interest and exchange rates might be needed to accommodate temporary shocks that could be both favorable and unfavorable. Also, adjustments of reserve money growth targets were often needed to accommodate significant changes in the structure of the financial system.

As for Kapur's suggestion that countries focus monetary policy management on a target rate of disinflation or the maintenance of a low, steady-state inflation rate, Cole said he had no problem with that. Moreover, he also agreed that fiscal policy was an essential requirement in most countries for making significant changes in the financial system. But he cautioned that if countries tried to introduce a treasury bill market before they had achieved any control over fiscal policy, they would destroy the bill market even more rapidly than they would destroy the banking system through fiscal laxity.

Finally, Cole noted, there were many different types of rural financial models besides the community-based lending ones. The Bank Rakyat Indonesian Unit Desas was not an example of a community-based lending system, but a government-owned bank that made loans to individuals, with strong incentives to repay on time. Furthermore, there were a lot of informal institutions in Africa that could be easily linked to the organized financial system in constructive and creative ways.

7

What Next for African Parastatal Enterprises?

John Nellis

IN CONTRAST TO the rest of the world, where the economic and financial weight of parastatal corporations is declining, parastatals in Africa still account for a large amount of economic activity (as measured by GDP), nonagricultural employment, and investment. It is certainly true that the total number of African public enterprises has fallen considerably over the past decade as more and more African governments have undertaken privatization and divestiture programs. The World Bank estimates that the total number of public enterprises in Africa has decreased by as much as a third in the past decade.[1] Nonetheless, because the vast bulk of African firms privatized have been small, low-value units, African parastatals remain highly important economic, financial, and social actors (see Figure 1).

The continuing large size would not be a problem if African parastatals were performing well—but they are not. All over the continent, parastatals have not lived up to the expectations of their creators and funders. Estimates are that African parastatals, even with the recent privatizations, still consume about 20 percent of available human and physical capital but contribute only about 10 percent to value added. Regrettably, examples of poor performance are not hard to find:

---

[1]See Oliver Campbell-White and Anita Bhatia, *Privatization in Africa* (Washington: World Bank, forthcoming, 1997).

Figure 1. African Parastatals Still Play a Major Role . . .

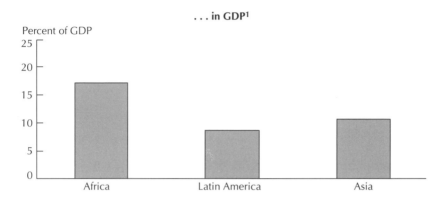

. . . in GDP[1]

. . . in Employment

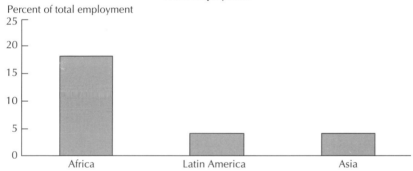

. . . in Gross Domestic Investment

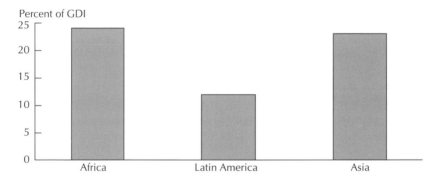

Source: Ahmed Galal and Mary Shirley, *Bureaucrats and Business: The Economics and Politics of Government Ownership,* World Bank Policy Research Report, Statistical Appendix (Washington: World Bank, 1995), pp. 268-97.
[1]1991 data for all three panels.

- In Kenya, government calculations show that the very large amount of capital invested in the parastatal sector over the past 30 years has yielded a rate of return of zero.
- In Ghana, the former Minister of Finance, speaking of parastatals, was quoted as saying in late 1994 that "huge sums of money are placed at the disposal of the public sector annually without the money yielding any dividend."
- In Burundi, over a three-year period, total net flows *from* the government to the parastatals averaged 12.5 percent of total government expenditure—and one should recall that the original justification of parastatals was that they would generate resources *for* the government, which would use the surplus to develop the rest of the economy. Now their persistently poor financial performance is justified for noneconomic reasons, such as employment generation and maintenance or regional development.
- A 1993 study of five African countries showed that total direct transfers to parastatals from governments ranged from 14 to 22 percent of government expenditures. Indirect flows—cheap credits, forgiveness of customs duties and taxes, and conversion of debt to equity—amounted to an additional 14 percent. In these cases, more than a quarter, and much more in some instances, of all government resources were used to support a small number of companies, employing a tiny fraction of these countries' workforces.
- In Uganda, subsidies in the 1990s have averaged $180 million a year—five times the spending on health—while the return flow to the government has been tiny. The sum transferred is equal to $6,000 per parastatal employee per year, over and above the wage bill.

The conclusions are all too evident: too many African parastatals still lose money, produce an insufficient quantity or a poor quality of product—sometimes both—and soak up human, physical, and financial resources that could be better applied to other, pressing societal needs. All this has long been known. The question is, what can be done to resolve these problems?

For at least 20 years, African countries, with and without donor assistance, have struggled to impose reforms and performance improvement measures on their parastatals. They have tried to:

- impose sound accounting, financial, and management information systems;
- clarify objectives and make commercial profitability a prime goal (entailing the elimination of noncommercial objectives, or the transparent costing-out and reimbursement of the firm for such activities);
- give managers the autonomy and incentives to achieve the assigned objectives (meaning the power to hire and fire, to set prices, to buy

inputs from least-cost suppliers, to locate plants according to commercial, not social criteria, etc.);

- create supervisory systems allowing the owner to hold management
accountable (setting out clear objectives, measuring management
performance in terms of the objectives, rewarding success, and
sanctioning persistent failure); and
- wherever possible, allow and encourage competition for the firm,
ideally without barriers to entry or exit.

But after years of effort along these lines (I personally have worked
on attempts to install such programs in Côte d'Ivoire, Kenya, Madasgas-
car, Niger, Senegal, Tanzania, and Togo)—and despite a few successes—
these reform packages have produced only modest or disappointing results. Why is this so? Because they tend to be only partially put in place,
and even when put in place, the packages tend not to endure—they do
not last. Thus, enterprise performance has rarely improved, or at least
not by enough to make a major difference. In particular, financial performance has remained weak, continuing to pose a great burden on
strained government budgets and on the banking system. Moreover, returns on government investment are woefully low and in some cases
negative and utilities still do not provide the efficient, reliable, cost-
effective services that are so necessary for increased investment and
growth.

Progress Report on Privatization

Disappointed with the mediocre results of reform, African governments began, in the mid-1980s—often prodded by donors and the international financial institutions—to turn to privatization. At first
glance, African privatization accomplishments look impressive. At least
2,000 African divestiture transactions were reported by the end of
1995, with a total value of more than $2 billion[2]—about one-third the
total estimated number of parastatals in the region. But 66 percent remain in the public portfolio. Moreover, progress has been limited to a
rather small number of countries; one-fourth of all reported transactions took place in just one country—Mozambique. If one adds
Angola, together they account for almost 40 percent of all divestitures.
If one also includes Ghana, Guinea, Kenya, Nigeria, Tanzania, and
Zambia—just eight countries account for two-thirds of all African
privatizations.

---

[2]Ibid., p. 56.

But much more important than the sheer numbers sold or retained is the fact that the majority of firms divested have been small and medium-sized companies. The big parastatals containing the bulk of state assets—electricity, telecommunications, mines, transport, ports, and refineries—tended until recently not to be touched by the privatization process (Figure 2), with a few notable exceptions such as SODECI, the water utility company in Côte d'Ivoire. Kenya offers an interesting case in point. Despite the efforts over the past ten years of various task forces, working groups, parliamentary commissions, and a parastatal reform and privatization program, the percentage of state assets divested has been very small; prior to 1996 and the partial sale of Kenya Airways to KLM, only one or two big companies were divested. The economic weight of the Kenyan state is only slightly less today than it was in 1985.

Figure 2. Sub-Saharan Africa Lags the World in Infrastructure Privatization

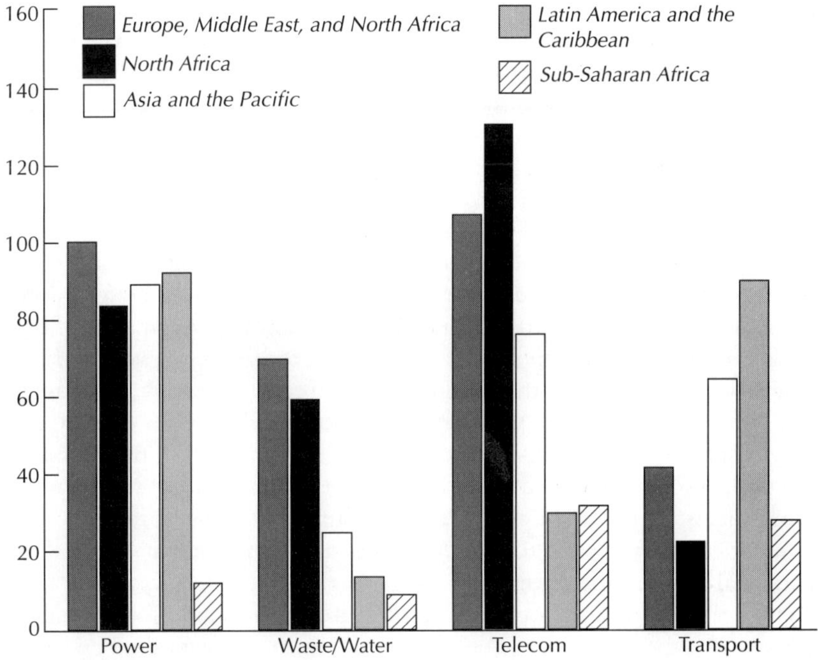

Source: Michael Kerf and Warrick Smith, *Privatizing Africa's Infrastructure: Promise and Challenge,* World Bank Technical Paper No. 337 (Washington: World Bank, 1996), p. 6.

Why has this been the case, not only in Kenya, but also in so many other African countries? The reasons are several.

- African governments are fearful that privatization will increase unemployment.
- African governments are fearful that the only buyers of divested firms will be foreigners, the domestic elite well-connected to the political system, or a particular ethnic group—and in many cases none of these are regarded as acceptable or optimal buyers.
- Some within African governments are fearful of losing their last bastion of patronage and resources (in terms of board directorships, access to cheap loans, employment possibilities for themselves and their constituents, cars, and other perks).
- Some governments are concerned that the privatization of African industries, and their subsequent operation in freer markets, would lead to the bankruptcy and liquidation of many of these companies. To put it starkly, there is fear that privatization would lead to the de-industrialization of the continent.
- Other African officials and observers think that while privatization in Africa may eventually be a good thing, they also think that it cannot and should not come about at the present time because of the absence or weakness of local capital markets, and the deficiencies of the court system, the customs office, the tax administrators, or other parts of the administrative system. This is something of a paradox in that perceived weaknesses of the public sector are used to justify keeping activities in that very same public sector.

Faced with these daunting obstacles and perceptions, what can be done to advance parastatal reform and privatization in Africa?

First, we—the African governments and the donor community—can *take steps to improve information.* Primarily, there must be a better, more transparent accounting of the financial and economic performance of the parastatal sector. If African populations knew precisely how weakly parastatals were performing, the amount of resources they were absorbing, and what activities were being forgone because of these poor operations, they would be much more likely to support reforms. And if investors and the population at large had more faith in the transparency of the transaction process, there would be more public support for privatization.

Second, we can work toward *better and more consistently applied policy.* Parastatal reform and divestiture do not take place in a vacuum: they flourish and pay off to society when the macroeconomic fundamentals are sound, when the framework for competition is established and enforced, and when the government shows itself to be a credible and reliable partner, providing investors with a stable, predictable business environment.

**Figure 3. New Forms of Infrastructure Privatization
Offer Varied Benefits**

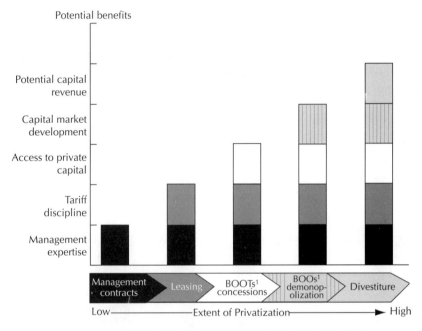

Source: Michael Kerf and Warrick Smith, *Privatizing Africa's Infrastructure:
Promise and Challenge,* World Bank Technical Paper No. 337 (Washington:
World Bank, 1996), p.10.
[1]For an explanation of BOOTs (Build-Own-Operate-Transfer) and BOOs
(Build-Own-Operate), see text footnotes 3.

Third, we must strive for *better functioning institutions.* Parastatal reform
and privatization, particularly of the large, problem-causing infrastructure firms, require that the government have the capacity to negotiate,
monitor, and enforce contracts, and where markets cannot be restructured to make competition a prospect, a modicum regulatory capacity
needs to be in place. This is easier said than done: developing such capacities will, in many instances, take quite a bit of time.

This is precisely why partial privatization—bringing in the private
sector as manager, financier, or part equity owner—is gaining so much
popularity in Africa in the last few years. Many governments know that
they acutely need efficiency improvements in the big parastatals, but
they feel they cannot be sold because of the fear of foreign domination,
combined with concerns about deficiencies in the country's regulatory
capacity. In these cases, the mechanisms of management contracts, leases,

Table 1. Infrastructure Privatization in Africa Takes Many Forms

Sector	Management Contract	Lease Central	Concession BOOT	Demonopolize BOO[1]	Divestiture
Water	Gabon Gambia Mali	Central African Republic Côte d'Ivoire Guinea South Africa Côte d'Ivoire Guinea			
Electricity	Gabon Gambia Ghana Guinea Guinea-Bissau Mali Rwanda Sierra Leone			Côte d'Ivoire Mozambique	
Telecom- munications	Benin Botswana Guinea Madagascar		Guinea-Bissau	Burundi Ghana Guinea Madagascar Mauritius Namibia Nigeria South Africa Tanzania Uganda Zaïre	Sudan
Railways	Cameroon Tanzania Togo	Burkina Faso Côte d'Ivoire Gabon Zaïre			
Airports	Togo	Benin Gabon Guinea Madagascar Mauritania	Cameroon Mali		
Ports	Sierra Leone	Cameroon Mozambique	Mali Mozambique	South Africa	

Source: Michael Kerf and Warrick Smith, *Privatizing Africa's Infrastructure: Promise and Challenge*, World Bank Technical Paper No. 337 (Washington: World Bank, 1996), p.19.
[1] For an explanation of BOOTs (Build-Own-Operate-Transfer) and BOOs (Build-Own-Operate), see text footnotes 3.

concessions, and "BOOTs" and "BOOs"[3] are becoming more widely used, and justifiably so (Figure 3).

Policy Prescriptions

The practical implications of this brief resumé are several. First, African governments should not hesitate to privatize those parastatals producing tradable products and operating in competitive, or potentially competitive, markets. To make this policy work requires dropping barriers to purchase by noncitizens or citizens of a supposedly "wrong" ethnic group. It also means avoiding unreasonable floor prices for companies being sold and writing off uncollectible debts that have long been disguised as assets. It will also mean accepting that some parastatals can neither be sold nor kept in the state portfolio, and that liquidation is the only rational solution.

Second, governments should search for all available ways to involve the private sector in the running of the infrastructure parastatals, in particular, the very largest ones with the greatest economic weight. This is starting to happen all over Africa; the process should be vigorously pursued (Table 1).

Neither of these general prescriptions will be easy. But both are essential if Africa is to rebound into sustained growth.

---

[3]BOOTs and BOOs are privatization mechanisms that are becoming increasingly popular. BOOT (Build-Own-Operate-Transfer) is a situation in which a long-term concession (normally between 20 and 40 years) is given to a private firm for the exploitation of a particular service or facility. The firm has the responsibility to finance, build, and operate the facility for a given period of time. The private firm also takes property title to the facility in the construction period and transfers it back to the government at the end of the long-term concession. This is often used in cases in which loan guarantees or collateral are required. BOO (Build-Own-Operate) is similar to BOOT, but in this case the property is not transferred back to the government at the end of the concession period.

Comments

Yasuo Yokoyama

Thank you, Mr. Nellis, for your informative speech. I would like to comment by drawing on my own experiences in Nairobi, Kenya, from 1988 to 1992, and in Johannesburg, South Africa, since 1994.

While I was in Kenya, I tried to grant Japanese overseas development assistance (ODA) to textile manufacturers (parastatals) that the government wanted to privatize, but in the end, this was not possible. I realized that what the textile parastatals really needed to do was to first reform their management and financial position to improve productivity—using Japanese ODA funds—and only then to proceed with privatization.

We should ask why the necessity of privatization of parastatals exists. As I understand it, the motivations are, first, to reduce government budget deficits, and second, to give economic incentives to the private sector to boost efficiency.

But how quickly should countries move on this front? My conclusion regarding sub-Saharan African countries is that *rapid* privatization will not produce the desired good results but instead only pose further difficulties for the business sector. In other words, I think countries should concentrate on adopting projects to solve many problems—such as the need for good business sense and a profit-minded approach—which should be implemented gradually over several years. Countries should also spend 50–100 years establishing sound economic fundamentals before embarking on privatizations.

Imagine a country with a GNP per capita of $100 and another country with a GNP per capita of $500 or more. You can easily see that there are big differences in what they should do over the next five years.

Countries with a GNP per capita of less than $500 should use overseas ODA funds to gradually improve their economic situation. Initial steps could involve improving telecommunications, railways, roads, airports, and seaport systems. In Asia, the Japanese government and the private sector successfully adopted such a step-by-step process, with the private sector only introducing their investment and finance once the economy had sharply improved, that is, reached a GNP per capita exceeding $500.

Next, think about the type of country that would have a GNP per capita of $500. From our experience, this type of country would be on the road to a stable political situation, together with gradual achievements in the areas of freedom and democracy. It would also be making progress in fiscal and monetary policy, especially in curbing foreign exchange and interest rate controls—moves that are critical for future successful privatizations. During this stage, management and technical staff should be trained, and competitive products introduced into the international market. After experiencing such progress—and only then—should a country consider privatizations, a further step in the maturing process.

How should the African countries best utilize Japanese ODA? My experience of eight years in Africa and a long time in the private sector suggests that what these countries need is water supply projects for health and irrigation reasons, road construction to assist economic activities, and education to improve management and technical skills. In these areas, the government and the private sector should cooperate with each other on every possible occasion.

We, together with the African people, should not insist on privatization as the sole solution. Rather, we should look for alternative ways and means to create an African paradise in the 21st century, the hope of our next generation.

8

Parastatal Reform and Privatization in Côte d'Ivoire

Jean-Claude Brou

FOLLOWING ITS INDEPENDENCE in 1960, Côte d'Ivoire opted for a liberal economy that was built around the agricultural sector, especially export crops such as coffee and cocoa, and that actively sought private foreign capital. This policy enabled the country to record a high sustained rate of growth—averaging 7 percent annually during the first 20 years following independence—with a GDP that increased more than 15-fold.

Faced with a desire to diversify the economic base and develop basic infrastructure, yet saddled with a weak domestic private sector, the government adopted a policy of actively supporting economic activity, particularly by creating a large number of public enterprises in almost all sectors: agriculture, industrial processing, distribution, the financial sector, and transportation, to name but a few. The government acted alone or jointly with domestic and foreign investors, as the need arose.

By 1977, there were 113 public enterprises, employing one-third of Côte d'Ivoire's labor force, using 27 percent of public investment resources, and receiving close to 40 percent of government loans. The high rate of economic growth, buoyed by the surge in international prices for the main export crops, favored the pursuit of this policy of active government participation in production activities. As a result, the number of public enterprises grew steadily year after year, reaching 140 by 1982. But economic trends would soon lead to a change in this policy.

Evaluation of the Parastatal Sector

By the early 1980s, Côte d'Ivoire's economic situation had deteriorated markedly with the unprecedented decline in world prices for its two main export crops, coffee and cocoa. The economic crisis pointed to significant structural rigidities as well as weaknesses in the management of the economy, which were reflected in a serious fiscal deficit, a high level of overall debt, an unprecedented decline in economic activity and per capita income, and a significant loss of competitiveness.

One of the main reasons for these difficulties was the inefficiency of the parastatal sector and its excessive weight in the economy. An evaluation of the entire parastatal sector in 1982–88 revealed that its total net profits over the period were about CFAF[1] 39 billion, despite total subsidies of CFAF 568 billion (including CFAF 165 billion for public and semipublic enterprises).[2] A more extensive analysis during the same period also revealed that:

- the subsector in which the government was *sole shareholder* had total net losses of CFAF 85 billion;
- the subsector in which the government was *majority shareholder* had total net losses of CFAF 10 billion; and
- in contrast, the subsector in which the government was *minority shareholder* had recorded a total profit of CFAF 134 billion.

Moreover, the subsector in which the government was sole shareholder paid the least taxes but received the most government transfers and subsidies. During the period 1989–91, direct government subsidies to parastatal sector enterprises totaled close to CFAF 330 billion, representing more than 20 percent of tax revenues for the same period.

Why did the public enterprises perform so poorly? The main reasons are the well-known factors mentioned above, which tend to explain the relatively lower economic efficiency of the public enterprises. I would mention in particular the weak management systems, very low productivity levels, a certain amount of rigidity in the regulation system, the existence of uncompetitive contracts, and the lack of effective controls within the enterprises.

The government tried to deal with the problem by attempting to reform the parastatal sector, as part of a number of structural adjustment programs it undertook in the 1980s. Several public enterprises were liq-

---

[1]US$1 = CFAF 302.95. This is the exchange rate at the end of 1988. After the devaluation in 1994, the exchange rate has hovered around US$1 = CFAF 500 during the period 1995–96.

[2]The parastatal sector includes public and semipublic enterprises, as well as autonomous public agencies *(Etablissements publics)*.

uidated, while others were merged; restructuring and rehabilitation programs were introduced; and economic and financial performance indicators were established. However, although a slight improvement was recorded, the results remained below par.

Overall Economic Performance

Of course, public enterprise reform efforts must be viewed in the context of what was happening to the economy as a whole. During the period 1988–93, per capita GDP declined steadily by an average of 5 percent a year, largely as a result of weak economic performance and a high population growth rate (about 3.8 percent). Furthermore, in 1993, macroeconomic imbalances reached unsustainable levels: the overall fiscal deficit was close to 13 percent of GDP, the balance of payments current account deficit stood at 11 percent of GDP, and outstanding external public debt was about 173 percent of GDP.

Following the 50 percent devaluation of the fixed parity of the CFA franc—the common currency of the seven members of the West African Economic and Monetary Union—with the French franc in 1994, the authorities undertook an ambitious stabilization and economic recovery program. The program included a series of budgetary and monetary measures, along with various structural measures aimed at bringing the economy back on the road to strong, sustainable economic growth, particularly by restoring its competitiveness.

It is essential to remember that the strategy adopted by the authorities was twofold: a more efficient use of public resources, notably by means of more consistent expenditures in the social sectors, such as education and health; and a greater role for the private sector in economic activity, particularly through privatization.

Foreign and domestic trade were broadly liberalized, nontariff barriers were almost totally eliminated, and the number of goods and services subject to price controls was significantly reduced. In addition, a new, more flexible labor code and an investment code were introduced to offer greater incentives. Various sectors of the economy were liberalized. The public enterprise sector was restructured, and a major privatization program was begun. As a result, economic performance in 1994 and 1995 was satisfactory to say the least. Economic growth stood at 1.8 percent in 1994 and rose to 7 percent in 1995—and should hold at that level in 1996. Inflation was reduced considerably, down to 7.7 percent in 1995 from 32 percent in 1994. The current account deficit was narrowed by 10 percentage points to 4 percent of GDP in 1995, and the overall budget deficit was reduced significantly, to less than 3.5 percent of GDP.

Restructuring Public Enterprises and Privatization

In the parastatal sector, the policy of the authorities has focused on two complementary aspects: completely restructuring the institutions and public enterprises that would remain in government hands, and divesting the government's interests in the productive sector through privatization.

Public Enterprise Reform

In this area, the primary objective was to boost the effectiveness of the enterprises, particularly by increasing management autonomy and improving the auditing and monitoring of their administration and financial and technical management. To this end, a detailed database on these enterprises was created, along with a system for reporting key financial indicators on a quarterly basis. In a general policy statement on the parastatal sector, the authorities reiterated the principle of strengthening internal and external controls of public enterprises and establishing financial equilibrium and profitability targets.

As a result, performance contracts are to be negotiated between the government and public enterprises. Measures to streamline the operations of public enterprises are to be introduced—including merit pay, monitoring of public enterprise investments and their consistency with the public investment program, monitoring of net bank credit to the parastatal sector, and elimination of cross-arrears between public enterprises. Moreover, specific restructuring plans have been prepared and implemented for the largest public enterprises.

Privatization

The government's most significant and successful efforts have taken place in the privatization program itself. This program affects about 60 enterprises and covers almost all economic sectors—including infrastructure sectors such as electricity, telecommunications, the railroad, petroleum, and agricultural processing.

The program was initiated in 1991 and stepped up significantly in 1994–95. Since 1991, 31 public enterprises have been privatized, generating CFAF 45 billion in revenue—which amounts to 7 percent of nontax revenue during the period. In addition, the privatizations allowed most of the enterprises concerned to undertake restructuring programs and become profitable again. These privatizations took place chiefly in the electricity, petroleum, railroad, and rubber processing sectors.

The privatized enterprises invested significant amounts in rehabilitation and renovation to benefit from the rising aggregate demand that resulted from the economic recovery that began in 1994. A recent survey of the major privatized enterprises reveals investment levels of over CFAF 58 billion in 1994–95, with investments of CFAF 115 billion forecast for 1996–98. Moreover, the improved general economic environment has enabled the privatized enterprises to increase the number of jobs created by more than 6 percent.

Thus, privatization has not only reduced the weight of these enterprises on the government by reducing subsidies but it has also contributed to public resources in the form of profits. The electricity sector, which went from a chronic deficit to a profit in the first year following privatization, is a good example of the advantages of privatization.

Indeed, whereas the public electricity company had recorded a high cumulative deficit with no returns to the state, privatization has enabled the company to show a cumulative net profit of CFAF 5.5 billion and to return almost CFAF 80.2 billion to the government in the form of royalties during 1991–94. This financial improvement—in part thanks to a bill collection rate of 98 percent, compared with 80 percent previously—was also accompanied by an improvement in the quality of service (notably, a reduction in the length of power cut per year and per client from 50 hours to about 20 hours).

Lessons on Privatization

When we consider what lessons can be drawn from the privatizations in Côte d'Ivoire, five essential points come to mind.

First, as in most countries that have implemented successful privatization programs, *a balanced macroeconomic environment is essential.* In the case of Côte d'Ivoire, the existence of an overvalued real effective exchange rate during 1987–93, along with fiscal imbalances and balance of payments disequilibria, constituted a serious barrier to the implementation of the privatization program. Between 1990 and 1993, only nine public enterprises were privatized, generating barely CFAF 4.5 billion in revenue.

However, following the realignment of the parity of the CFA franc, and the implementation of budgetary and monetary measures—as well as measures to liberalize the economy and increase competition—the privatization program took off. During 1994–95, 22 enterprises were privatized, bringing in close to CFAF 40 billion in revenue, or more than nine times the revenue mobilized in 1990–93. In 1995, privatization receipts reached CFAF 32 billion, or 3.5 percent of total tax revenue. Estimates for 1996 give privatization receipts of about CFAF 40 billion, equivalent to 4 percent of total tax revenue.

Thus, an appropriate macroeconomic framework, by altering the expectations of potential investors, especially as regards the profitability of investments, is key to the success of a program of structural reforms, and especially a privatization program.

Second, *privatization must take place in the context of a competitive market* so as to ensure an optimal allocation of resources. However, in some sectors, especially infrastructure sectors such as electricity, the size of the market in developing countries does not yet allow for the existence of a competitive market. In Côte d'Ivoire, to take this into account, an agreement was signed between the government and the private operator of the electricity network defining their respective responsibilities, especially on establishment of the rates.

Third, *privatization must have full political support as well as the support of a majority of the people*. Political support is a decisive factor for a privatization program, especially when the targeted enterprises are deemed to be strategic or closely linked to the national interest—such as in the electricity, telecommunications, or other infrastructure sectors. In Côte d'Ivoire, this political support has resulted from the endorsement of privatization by the highest levels of government and the passing of a law by the National Assembly. Furthermore, particular attention must also be paid to the perception of the role played by foreign investors purchasing national public enterprises. In Côte d'Ivoire, the solution was to encourage partnerships between domestic and foreign private operators.

Public support, for its part, is closely linked to what might be called the democratization of the privatization process. Privatization is unlikely to succeed if it is perceived to be a way for a minority, be it domestic or foreign, to appropriate the public enterprises. Public support was not achieved in Côte d'Ivoire until the first privatization operations on the stock exchange allowed a large number of small domestic investors to purchase shares in the privatized companies, particularly the electricity company. Indeed, almost systematic reservation of a portion of shares for small national investors was a critical element. Through such participation, privatization becomes a reality and social acceptance becomes possible.

Another aspect of public support that should be mentioned is the improvement in the quality of service following privatization. For example, after an initial negative reaction, the privatization of the electricity sector was accepted, mainly because of the improved service that followed.

Fourth, *the prior definition of a clear, transparent, and rigorous process* is also a prerequisite for successful privatization. Any deviation from these principles, however small, can slow down and even obstruct the privatization in two ways:

- the perception that the "deck is stacked" can discourage some potential investors; and
- a very negative public reaction to a perceived lack of rigor and transparency in the process—and concomitantly, an "undervaluing" of the government's shares and assets—can also slow down the process.

Fifth, *it is essential to be flexible and pragmatic* in implementing privatization. Despite the existence of a predetermined, prioritized schedule, the privatization program must be implemented flexibly, taking into account the interests of the investors. In Côte d'Ivoire, the privatization operations in the rubber processing and railroad sectors were begun at the specific request of investors interested in developing these sectors.

Conclusion

The existence of efficient public enterprises and privatization are today an international reality. The globalization of the economy makes the implementation of a privatization program inevitable. If well designed and well implemented, privatization can help developing countries improve the performance of their economies. In Côte d'Ivoire, despite the difficulties encountered, the process has enabled the country to make important advances in the area of structural reform, particularly in the public enterprise sector. It is expected that the privatization process will be completed in 1997.

9

Parastatal Reform and Privatization in Mali

Soumaïla Cissé

M ALI SUFFERED a severe economic and financial crisis in the early
1980s due to natural phenomena and, in particular, the implementation of inappropriate policies. This crisis caused stark imbalances:
low growth combined with a high population increase; structural imbalances in government finance and the balance of payments; and inadequate savings to meet major investment needs.

Now, after several adjustment programs supported by the international community—and I would like to take this opportunity to thank
the international community, on behalf of the Malian people, for its
continuing assistance—we are seeing positive results. The various program reviews have shown that:

- government finance is improving;
- the economic growth rate has increased from 2.3 percent in 1994
  to 6 percent in 1995;
- inflation is being controlled after the change in the parity of the
  currency in 1994;
- budgetary revenue is 13 percent higher than financial program
  projections;
- the external debt is being fully serviced;
- budgetary expenditure is being contained;
- the economic environment for the private sector has improved, as
  have the legal conditions under which it operates; and
- the government has totally or partially divested 44 public sector
  enterprises.

Certainly, the dawn of the Third Republic, after the first multiparty elections in Mali in 1992, was a decisive turning point in the political, economic, and social development of the Malian people.

Where have we come from? During the political and social unrest of March 1991, the productive base and the economic and financial administrations were devastated, and the very survival of the state was in jeopardy. Economic and financial losses were estimated at more than CFAF 30 billion—that is, some 5 percent of the nation's wealth. Moreover, the authority of the government was eroded to the point where the security forces could no longer perform their functions and tax evasion was rampant.

In 1992, the emergence of a multiparty democracy immediately broadened the framework for consensus-building in public management. Political parties, labor unions, and civil associations proliferated. We even had an association of "victims of structural adjustment." But interest group demands became more strident, with everyone clamoring for everything at once. And during these years, the education crisis—which continues to seriously threaten our future—reached a peak in 1993/94 with the closing of all schools. Students at all levels were making extreme demands, the most revealing one being their demand for a "perennial scholarship."

The armed conflict in the northern part of the country continued until March 27, 1996, when, in an outburst of national unity, a "flame of peace" burned more than 3,000 weapons surrendered by the various warring factions. This social peace must still be consolidated, however, and the upcoming legislative and presidential elections of 1997 are fueling a new bout of protests.

Clearly our work is far from over, and the pitfalls are many. But we have seen promising results—results that are a consequence of both the profound change in the political context and the constantly evolving macroeconomic environment. In order for us to continue the structural reforms, and thus to fuel progress, support from our development partners is required.

I would now like to turn to Mali's experience in the following areas: mobilizing budgetary revenue, reforming the financial sector, and reforming the nonfinancial sector.

Mobilizing Domestic Resources

Achieving a lasting improvement in the government's budgetary situation is an essential component of Mali's adjustment strategy. But it was not until 1994—despite many earlier adjustment programs—that the domestic resources mobilized finally exceeded the financial objectives of the program, a new trend that was consolidated in 1995.

What happened was that, in response to a frank diagnostic study, the financial authorities (including customs officials) drew up and implemented a plan of action. The initiatives included:

- an ambitious investment program to rehabilitate and construct premises to house the tax assessment and tax collection services;
- an on-the-job training and awareness program for the various categories of staff;
- an appropriate communications campaign to restore tax compliance and to improve the image of tax collection officials in the eyes of the public;
- an international import verification company to improve the monitoring of transactions at customs;
- a reduction in the size of the staff of the financial administrations (mainly involving those that did not have the required training);
- a major effort to simplify taxation and stabilize collection procedures; and
- a system for weekly monitoring of public revenue and expenditure performance in the Ministry of Finance and Commerce.

This close monitoring of the adjustment program, involving all the senior officials of the Ministry, is the cornerstone of the system that has made such a good performance possible. The Bretton Woods institutions have noted these results, which demonstrates that the efforts made have not been in vain. Indeed, these efforts will be continued.

Financial Sector Reform

In a monetary union such as the one to which Mali belongs—the West African Economic and Monetary Union (WAEMU)—financial sector reform is still quite a sensitive issue, as the economies in the area adjust at different rates. Reform of economic policy instruments and regulations must be the subject of regional dialogue. However, the main problem remaining is to restore the confidence of the private sector.

Where do we stand? In the mid-1980s, government cash flow difficulties and poor management of the savings bank and postal checking system led to a freezing of the assets of small savers. The result was a mistrust of the banking system. Reform took a long time to complete: first, it sought to improve the security of private funds in the financial system by breaking the links between these funds and the financing of the public deficit, and then it sought to make these assets liquid.

The determining factor in the restoration of private transactors' confidence lies in the fact that the government has had "visible" financial surpluses. Transactors have found that payment delays by the treasury have been much reduced and that domestic arrears have been paid in accordance with the announced program.

More recently, the financial crisis that affected the Meridien Group in 1994 has shown the government's ability to react and to protect the interests of the private sector. This action helped strengthen the government's credibility and improve confidence in the banking system.

Even so, neither the modern banking sector nor the informal sector (savings and loans, tontines, etc.) fund the national economy as they should, despite the fact that there is abundant liquidity. There are still blockages, and the guarantees and procedures required are still cumbersome.

With the World Bank's help, we in Mali are looking at restructuring the banking and financial system with a view to improving bank intermediation and promoting investment. We are seeking to replace the government at the core of the financial system by issuing treasury bills, for which there is currently a demand in the private sector.

Reforms in Nonfinancial Sectors

Successful macroeconomic reform is conditional upon reforms in the nonfinancial sectors. Urgent action must be taken in the supply of goods and services to the poorest segments of the population. The scope and variety of needs create a problem of setting priorities, a crucially important step in stabilization.

In the area of *education,* no country has been able to develop with a school enrollment rate of less than 50 percent; this rate was 30 percent for Mali in 1994. With the support of a number of partners, including the World Bank, we have implemented an accelerated development program for basic education, which includes reforming educational practices to increase the number of students and improve the efficiency of human resources and teacher training. At the same time, a major program to build and outfit classrooms is under way.

In the area of *infrastructure,* the sectoral project that has just been put into effect will make it possible to rationalize the transport system, improve its financial performance, and make better use of and expand existing capacity.

In the area of *health,* the primary health care policy coming out of the Bamako initiative, recommended by the World Health Organization for all countries in Africa, has been satisfactorily implemented through the rural clean water and population project. Structural reforms in the area of public health are being completed with the liberalization of the practice of medical professions and the sale of drugs. The existing measures seek to make essential drugs widely available and to increase the number of community health centers, in the context of improving cost recovery. These steps will also make available more than 1,700 wells and watering places in areas where water supply needs are most acute.

The natural resource management project will allow farmers and local communities to permanently manage their land themselves. These communities first define their program, then the project provides them with financial assistance. These programs include a variety of activities: building dykes, supplying drinking water, constructing granaries, improving roads, and so on.

The public works job creation project made it possible to speed up urban sanitation, improve the performance of small enterprises engaged in public works, and create more than 35,000 jobs using labor-intensive techniques.

In the area of *privatization,* there are currently still 24 enterprises that are majority or entirely state-owned, and the government holds a minority share in 16 others.

We are trying to intensify the efforts made to date to increase the effectiveness of public services, reduce the burden of the public enterprise sector on the national budget, and broaden the participation of the private sector in all areas of economic life. The National Assembly requests that it be consulted concerning each enterprise involved in the privatization program. The established program may, therefore, undergo some modifications, which the government must bear in mind in its reform program.

Nonetheless, let me stress, in particular, the achievements in rural development through the Malian textile development company—Compagnie Malienne pour le Développement des Textiles (CMDT)—under successive projects supported by development partners.

Through the CMDT, wide-ranging five-year rural development programs were implemented. Today, it is unanimously acknowledged that this substantial financial support, amounting to a total of SDR 80.3 million, has been a success and has helped to make the CMDT efficient. The 1990 World Bank evaluation report says that the CMDT, through its competence and efficiency in project management and execution, is the top-performing cotton company in West Africa.

The three five-year programs completed have made it possible to:
- expand cereal production, including corn, in which Mali has become self-sufficient;
- promote village associations;

- conduct literacy programs in villages;
- supply inputs and extend loans to farmers;
- protect the environment by combating soil erosion; and
- develop and maintain rural roads and sources of drinking water.

Mali is now the second-largest African producer of cotton and we expect to be the first by the end of this decade. We now have the necessary capacity and are striving for excellence in managing the sector and in maintaining the industrial plant.

Conclusions

Mali is aware that it is an integral part of an economic and monetary union. The success of the economic policy conducted in the different countries will determine whether the present results are consolidated. The establishment of the WAEMU in 1994 will be a major asset for our future.

The outlook could be even better if a lasting solution were found to the debt problem, if external assistance were better coordinated, and if program design and management took better account of the changing environment resulting from the democratization of the political system, program "ownership," and popular participation. Furthermore, it is essential for programs to be longer in duration so that their real, long-term prospects can materialize.

I believe that this is the only way for us to be able to board the train of human progress. Just as the inevitability of underdevelopment is a fallacy, so too is development not merely a matter of chance but a well thought out and managed process.

The ultimate goal of our action is to rid our people of the scourge of poverty, which is holding us back. This is a noble ambition, and we are grateful that this august gathering shares it.

General Discussion

Accelerating Public Enterprise Reforms

Edouard Luboya of Zaïre, a representative of the private sector in Zaïre, began the discussion by suggesting that the presentations from Côte d'Ivoire and Mali showed that there was no point in deferring privatization—a rebuttal to some who had advised that countries spend decades establishing sound economic fundamentals, as Asian countries had done, before embarking on privatization. Moreover, Luboya argued, Zaïre's experience in recent years pointed to the same conclusion about timing. With the country in crisis, the private sector had stepped in and taken the initiative, particularly in the area of infrastructure. As a result, Zaïre now had more than 20 airlines covering the entire national territory, with some of them also able to service international routes. Cellular phones were now available, with prices dropping. And many large companies had training centers with physicians and modern equipment. All of those developments demonstrated that countries could move very swiftly on privatization. At the same time, however, Luboya noted that further progress had been inhibited by the frequent tension between the private and public sectors—a legacy of a misunderstanding that had existed ever since independence—but hopefully those disputes could soon be resolved.

Chérif Bichara of Chad noted that his country, too, had made a great deal of progress on privatization. Chad had decided in 1972 to get the state out of about 50 public and parastatal companies, and it had managed to privatize about half of those, without any major difficulties. His advice to others was fourfold:

- Policymakers needed to communicate the goals of the privatization programs and secure the support of the whole country—particularly unions, parliaments, and political parties.
- Policymakers needed to arrange for staff of the company slated for privatization to be associated with the future company. In Chad, when companies were privatized, 10 percent of the shares were reserved for staff, making them shareholders and thus giving them a say in the management of the company.
- Policymakers should ensure a certain amount of transparency, such as in the call for bids. Otherwise, it would be difficult to build enthusiasm for the initiative, as people would be suspicious about who stood to profit.
- Policymakers should proceed cautiously when it came to privatizing the banking sector, as participants needed to build trust and act with discretion. Indeed, this was the one sector where Chad had run into difficulties with privatization. Banks could not be privatized with a snap of the fingers—meaning that it was not always possible to meet World Bank deadlines.

Responding to John Nellis's statement that Africa was lagging behind other regions on privatization, *Joseph Tsika* of the Congo also insisted that Africa was keen to move forward on privatization in recognition of the fact that lame duck parastatals were costing the governments enormous sums of money. In Congo, for example, 150 companies had been slated for action in 1994. Since then, 53 had been liquidated, and the 6 largest were being privatized, thanks to a World Bank credit. So the fact that there were obstacles did not mean that the governments were dragging their feet. That said, it was important to recognize that there was still a certain amount of hesitation on the part of private partners and workers who would need to enter into the privatization process. He asked Jean-Claude Brou to what extent Côte d'Ivoire was able to engage the social partners, such as the unions, in the process, as the Congo's main problem had been wildcat strikes, largely for political reasons.

As for Yasuo Yokoyama's comment on taking sufficient time for the process, Tsika asked how countries could hold off privatizing and yet improve their economic fundamentals by not supporting inefficient parastatals. In some instances, that would mean not supporting entire sectors. People would wake up one morning with no telephone, no water, and no electricity. Moreover, donors were saying that if recipients did not privatize by a certain date, disbursements would stop. How were the financing gaps to be filled? It was a vicious circle.

In response to Tsika's question on involving labor, *Brou* noted that in all the privatizations, about 5 percent of the shares were put aside for employees. The private operators that purchased the enterprises had to put those shares aside for the employees and create common funds for them. The employees were also informed from the start about the type of approach that would be taken in the privatization process and kept abreast of developments, even though they did not actually take part in the negotiations.

Joseph Kinyua of Kenya underscored the progress Kenya had made on privatization in recent years, pointing to its commitment in its Policy Framework Paper to sharply reduce the public sector over the next three years, leaving only a few strategic parastatals. In the short term, improved efficiency of investment should become clear, and in the medium term, the impact on the overall economy should become evident. He also took issue with Nellis's statement that the economic weight of the Kenyan state was only slightly less today than it had been in 1985. Kinyua emphasized that there had been a substantial improvement in terms of the government's burden arising from either subsidies or resource transfers. Moreover, debt payments on behalf of the parastatals had dropped to 1.5 percent of government revenue from 5 to 6 percent three or four years ago.

Ben Ibe of Nigeria also pointed to recent successes in his country in privatization and streamlining of public enterprises but conceded that progress was not at the level that the World Bank would want. In some industries—such as airways, shipping, railways, and steel—enterprises were so run down that no one was interested in buying them. In a few other industries—such as power, hydrocarbons, and telecommunications—huge foreign debts needed to be settled before interested buyers would proceed. Then there was the question of appeasing labor and interest groups before companies could be put up for privatization. What advice could the World Bank offer?

Mary Muduuli of Uganda, emphasizing the need for Africa to better manage structural reforms, seconded the notion that a major obstacle to privatization was a lack of public awareness of its benefits. She also noted that, similarly, governments had failed to sell civil service reform, inadequately preparing the public and especially the affected employees. Uganda was only now waking up to the need to use advertisements in the media and drama shows to explain the advantages of privatization, an important step in ensuring smooth implementation and participation of citizens in the future ownership arrangements for the privatized enterprises.

Kwesi Botchwey of Ghana observed that as soon as governments announced that they planned to privatize enterprises, the immediate question asked was who would be the buyers. Opposition parties took advantage of the situation by telling the public that the government was abandoning them. To the extent that notion took hold among support-

ers of privatization, it tended to undermine the process—in part because it was accompanied by the reality that privatization would involve
reengineering and downsizing, meaning job losses. Thus, communicating clearly the benefits of privatization to the public was important—
even if they were not immediate.

In response, *Nellis* agreed that privatization was inevitably an intensely
political process, a problem that could not be swept under the rug. It
raised serious issues, such as the impact on labor, the nationality—or
sometimes even the ethnicity—of the purchaser, and the use by opposition parties of the privatization programs to advance their own political interests.

Nellis conceded that privatization often negatively affected labor in
the short term, although he was very pleased to hear of many instances
where privatization had actually led to an increase in employment. But
the sad fact of the matter was that many of the enterprises were over-
staffed, with a key feature of their poor performance being excess employment. What advice could the World Bank offer? The institution
had found that successful privatization programs around the world had
usually been associated with programs of severance packages, sometimes more generous than required by law in order to entice people to
accept the programs. That had been the case in Argentina, as well as in
other Latin American countries, where privatization had gone forward
at a rapid rate. Perhaps what African countries needed was a trade
union for the unemployed—those individuals whose interests were
going to be advanced by liberalization. After all, the data suggested that
the private sector created jobs, while the public sector only maintained
them.

Turning to the need for public relations at an early stage of privatization, he noted that that was something the international financial institutions had previously neglected—by viewing privatization as a technical, rather than a political and social, problem. And in their technical
response, they had overlooked the need for governments to use every
means at their disposal to alert people to the costs of inactivity, the costs
of poor performance, and the benefits of privatization. Even so, it was
true, as Botchwey had commented, that the costs were immediate and
focused, while the benefits were long term and diffused, making privatization a difficult sell for politicians.

Yasuo Yokoyama responded to several speakers who had taken issue
with a long time-horizon for reforms by citing Mozambique's recent
efforts to privatize the CFM, the national railway. Although the deal remained to be finalized, it appeared that only about 30 percent of the
shares would be left in Mozambique hands, with the remainder going
to foreigners (e.g., in the United Kingdom and South Africa). Yokoyama

questioned whether that could be called an optimal form of privatization. By contrast, Japan had considered the privatization of its railway company for many years before finally, a few years ago, launching a divestiture, a strategy that proved to be quite successful.

Enhancing the Effectiveness of External Assistance

10

World Bank– and IMF-Supported Programs: A Burkino Faso Perspective

Zéphirin Diabré

IN THE LATTER HALF of the 1970s and the early 1980s, most African countries, like other developing countries, were hit hard by the negative effects of trends in the international economic environment—particularly oil shocks, economic recession in the industrial countries, the steep rise in international interest rates, and the drop in raw materials prices. The impact of these exogenous shocks was intensified by the ineffective economic and financial policies that had gained currency in most of these countries. The convergence of these factors led to sizable and growing financial disequilibria (both internal and external), high inflation (except in the CFA franc zone countries), and economic recession. Structural weaknesses and the devastating effects of drought, particularly in the Sahelian region, made matters worse.

Thus, between 1965 and 1985, the average annual growth rate of GDP per capita was less than 1 percent for Africa, as opposed to 2.5 percent for Latin America, over 3 percent for North Africa, and just under 5 percent for East Asia and the Pacific.

Faced with these burgeoning economic and financial problems, a number of African countries—especially in the 1980s—embarked upon structural adjustment programs supported by the IMF and the World Bank. I

Zéphirin Diabré was not able to attend the seminar, but submitted this paper.

would like to now review our experience with these programs, starting with preparation, then content and acceptance, and finally social impact.

Preparation of IMF and World Bank Programs

As the adjustment programs prepared for Africa are the target of fairly harsh criticism, some lessons should be drawn and proposals made. The ideas concern three problem areas: the political economy of adjustment, beneficiary/donor relationships, and the link between adjustment and long-term development.

Political Economy of Adjustment

First, *the "ownership" of programs by the countries concerned is necessary:* adjustment programs should be about what countries *can do* and not what the World Bank and the IMF *want them to do.* The top priority should be participation in the design process; defining programs should involve more than exchanges between IMF and World Bank staff and government authorities. If the participants in development, in all their diversity, are not committed to the adjustment program, it is destined to fail.

Second, *the political marketing of adjustment is required.* For a number of reasons, the word adjustment elicits a type of psychological rejection in sub-Saharan Africa that should be corrected through constant efforts to explain and increase awareness. This approach is all the more necessary as the democracy movement has introduced African societies to the coexistence of several branches of government (executive, legislative, and judicial), each a participant in the decision-making process. Economic reforms and political liberalization sometimes seem to be at odds.

Third, *a regional approach to adjustment should be taken.* The trend toward regional integration is very strong in Africa, as the recent formation of the West African Economic and Monetary Union (WAEMU) demonstrates. It is absolutely essential, therefore, that programs take into account the trends that influence a country's overall picture.

Fourth, *programs must be custom tailored,* despite the strong temptation to formulate policies believed to apply to all countries that has long existed. As each country is a case apart, there are specific intrinsic factors that should be taken into account in the formulation of each program.

Beneficiary/Donor Relationships

Another problem area is the relationship between beneficiaries and donors when it comes to the assistance expected from the financial community to carry out planned reforms. The expected improvement in the current system will require two items in particular.

First, the *approach to conditionality should be changed.* The pace and sequence of reforms should be adapted to each country's specific capabilities and constraints with the conditionality more exacting in the long term and less formalistic in the short term. The conditionality should include general agreements on economic policy, based on a medium-term program in which specific measures are but one component. Flexibility should also be a factor, so that economic policy can be adjusted to accommodate changes in the national or international situation. It is better to base the conditionality of a program on the country's commitment and determination than on specific instruments or results.

Second, *disbursements should be prompter.* Experience has invariably shown that the amount of a disbursement is a determinant of the policy's success. There are, unfortunately, numerous examples where the assistance expected from the financial community does not—for complicated reasons related to procedures, work methods, or disagreement among donors—arrive at the most opportune moment.

Adjustment and Long-Term Development

The problems inherent in the relationship between adjustment and long-term development take on a critical dimension in sub-Saharan Africa, for the simple reason that this link is not perceived to exist for the recipient countries. The general impression is that the emphasis is on restoring macroeconomic equilibria at the expense of bona fide development. Planning for the future, which is an essential component of any long-term approach, is given short shrift in the adjustment programs.

Reforms often seem focused on regulating trade patterns, to the detriment of the overall growth of supply. This is true of agriculture, for example, where most of the reforms supporting sectoral programs have emphasized marketing problems without considering the need to provide transactors with resources to increase production. This is also true of every plan for the liberalization of domestic and foreign trade, where it is only too obvious that the primary concern—the ability to compete internationally—has not been addressed.

Content and Acceptance of Reforms

The reforms recommended in World Bank and IMF programs vary as to content and pose more or less similar acceptance problems.

Reforms targeting the public sector (public finances, civil service, and public enterprises) undoubtedly have the largest number of problems from the standpoint of acceptance. However, reforms affecting the external sector or involving changes in the legal and regulatory framework (exchange adjustments, the deregulation of imports, trade and price liberalization, or creation of incentive systems) are perceived in direct proportion to the economic antagonism they create or their potential for upsetting the status quo.

Public Sector Reforms

The public finances of African countries undergoing adjustment are often in a general state of deterioration, characterized by chronic revenue shortfalls (revenue collection is somewhat problematic in Africa) and difficulty in containing expenditure.

On the revenue side, efforts to broaden the tax base have been at the center of all the tax and customs reforms, and the results of these reforms have been positive overall—whether in terms of taxes at the border (lowering of customs duties) or domestic taxes (taxation of previously exempt sectors and introduction of a value-added tax). Having said that, we should acknowledge that introducing value-added taxes (VATs) and taxation of the informal sector are some of the fiscal reforms that have had at times negative consequences or have been difficult to implement. The VAT, when it is first introduced in the African economic framework, creates instant confusion for local experts, who are little acquainted with it. Informal sector taxation is complicated by the sector's elusive nature, its lack of public-spiritedness, and the difficulty of assessing its real activity.

Unquestionably, the most difficult type of public finance reform involves rationalizing expenditure. The necessity of this rationalization is obvious, as the African countries have, over the course of a decade, acquired spending habits sometimes out of proportion to their real ability to pay or to the exigencies of bona fide development.

But it is the pace of reform—more so than the objective—that sometimes causes a problem, owing to the painful consequences that these restrictive practices can have, especially in the social sphere or in terms of military security. On the latter point, it seems obvious that the burden of military expenditure still weighs too heavily on the distribution of resources in the African countries and is one of the most sensitive elements in the expenditure rationalization equation.

When African countries embark upon adjustment, their civil services are generally weighed down by not only sheer size—the excessive number of employees—but also a financial burden, with a large share of revenue going to the remuneration of the civil service itself.

Obviously, this creates a problem. But the usual solution—a drastic re-duction in the size of the civil service—while inevitable, poses a certain number of problems:

- the social function of civil service wages is severely diminished by downsizing or forced departures;
- the possibility of retraining those who leave is very limited and eventually leads them either to try to return or to join the ranks of the discontented, which creates instability;
- much of the supply of labor exists because of the attractiveness of civil service wages; and
- the departure of certain individuals deprives the government of the experience or expertise it needs to fully accomplish its purpose, which leads to problems involving capabilities.

The subject of the poor management of public enterprises is raised in every assessment concerning the African continent. Every country, it turns out, is a poor manager, but this situation takes on a special mean-ing in developing countries, where the question of capabilities remains unresolved. Viewed from this perspective, the recommended withdrawal of the government from public enterprises operating in the competitive sector is the best solution. To date, the privatization programs launched here and there in Africa have yielded uneven results, for reasons related to procedural transparency, the climate of repression, social and political pressures, or the weakness of the local private sector. Even so, the trend toward government divestiture of public enterprises operating in the competitive sector—while it entails the painful expedient of reorgani-zation and massive downsizing—is one that ought to be reinforced to enable the African countries to turn their attention to more vital tasks.

Reforms of the External Sector and the Regulatory Framework

In this area, price liberalization and the deregulation of imports are among the most difficult reforms to implement because labor and man-agement view it as giving free rein to inflation. Price liberalization is widely criticized, particularly in its early phase. But it is important to re-alize that this hostility, coming especially from union organizations, is strongest where the basic necessities of the majority are concerned.

As for deregulation of imports, sometimes state-controlled productive sectors—especially when there are clear opportunities for "rent seek-ing"—take a dim view of the opening of borders, which, for them, is synonymous with fierce competition. While it is not possible, in princi-ple, to give in to demands for limits or quotas, a look at the facts reveals that the subject of liberalization and competitiveness must be handled very delicately. Unfortunately, the feeling is entrenched that adjustment programs emphasize the former without providing sufficient resources to attain the latter. Only certain countries, such as Côte d'Ivoire, have been able to implement a program guaranteeing a certain level of competitiveness for their industries. Certainly, the best reforms involve the largest number of individuals and entities through innovative, participatory approaches. Knowledge of how to manage the entire political and social dimension of adjustment is needed.

Social Impact of Adjustment

Is not the debate concerning the social impact of adjustment in Africa skewed from the start? Because, in theory, the objective of programs supported by the IMF and the World Bank is initially to curb demand, these institutions are blamed for Africa's difficult social problems (health, education, access to drinking water, etc.). In reality, such a generalization can be extremely injurious to the pursuit of reforms. Examining this question leads us to consider the social impact of economic reforms and Burkina Faso's experience with the social aspect of adjustment.

Social Impact of Economic Reforms

Programs supported by the IMF and the World Bank are generally aimed at curbing demand and boosting supply, but while the reduction of demand is generally a short-term proposition, the recovery of supply takes time. Moreover, poverty is exacerbated in the interval.

What are the social impacts of specific policies? First, IMF-supported adjustment programs ordinarily limit the growth of total credit as part of the *monetary and credit policy*. As a result, the position of the largest enterprises can be strengthened at the expense of the smallest, and the poor working in small enterprises in the informal sector can be prevented from increasing their productive capacity. In addition, an overall limit on credit can have a negative, short-term impact on employment and real output, particularly when wages and nominal prices are rigid. This causes serious harm to certain segments of the poor, as the least-skilled members of low-income groups are usually the first to be fired when total employment shrinks.

Second, *price liberalization* measures are aimed at strengthening incentives and encouraging a more efficient distribution of resources. But even if these measures are justified in the short term, they have an impact on the least-advantaged populations, who benefited from administered prices.

Third, *labor market policies* are generally intended to preserve and expand employment by easing labor market rigidities. Particular emphasis is given to wage moderation policies and measures aimed at increasing job and wage flexibility. In the short term, these measures prove to be a difficult test for workers who have steady jobs in the formal sector. Moreover, a contraction in formal sector employment is generally accompanied by an increase in the supply of labor in the informal sector, which reduces the real income of the poor working in the informal sector. Unemployment cuts off not only the income of the poor in the short term but also their chances of finding long-term employment.

Fourth, turning to *exchange rate policies,* most adjustment programs come into being when there is a chronic imbalance in the external sector, which is often remedied by devaluing the exchange rate. When the factors of production are fixed, this leads in the short term to a rise in prices, dealing a severe blow to the poor.

Finally, regarding *fiscal policies,* all adjustment programs seek to bring about a significant reduction in the budget deficit, to diminish domestic imbalances and boost savings. The programs thus emphasize moderating expenditures and increasing revenues, but the measures generally involve a reduction in the wage bill, fewer subsidies, and the reorganization of public enterprises through privatization, liquidation, and so on—all of which translates into job losses in the short term.

Social Aspect of Adjustment in Burkina Faso

From the first adjustment program (1991–93) to the current one (1996–98), the social aspect of adjustment has been taken into account in Burkina Faso. This aspect figures prominently in our Policy Framework Paper.

• Since 1991, only the priority sectors of education, health, and financial administration (responsible for administering the Structural Adjustment Loan) have been authorized to hire additional staff and these sectors have also received the requisite budget appropriations since that date.

• A poverty profile study was conducted and the findings are now available—facilitating well-targeted action for accompanying measures.

• Liberalization of the rice trade was postponed because rice is a consumer staple; similarly, the profit margin control was left in place to protect consumers from the possibility of exorbitant price increases.

• To mitigate the effects of devaluation, a policy on the distribution of essential and generic medicines is being implemented with the support of the country's development partners.

Conclusion

Several recommendations can be made to increase the chances of success of adjustment programs in Africa.

First, *the strategic view of development should be internalized*—a process that begins with the preparation by national leaders of the draft adjustment programs to be negotiated with the IMF and the World Bank. The process is strengthened by involving the general public in the adjustment process through explanations.

Second, *poverty reduction should be the primary objective* of programs in Africa. This can be accomplished by increasing incomes (particularly in rural areas), strengthening support for the private sector, and allocating budget resources more efficiently to benefit the social sectors.

Third, we not only believe that *the shift in the approach of adjustment programs toward recognition of the social dimension is laudable,* but also hope that this process will be continued so as to reduce conditionality.

Fourth, *future programs in Africa will have greater chances of success if they are understood by the populations concerned,* which presupposes the preparation of programs by national leaders and involvement of the general public through large-scale, democratic debates.

Finally, *adjustment should henceforth have a regional dimension,* which would avoid the duplication of effort in individual countries, given the similarity of situations, and help to incorporate the political will expressed by the African countries to create larger and more viable regional economic areas.

11

World Bank– and IMF-Supported Programs: A Zambian Perspective

Jacob Mwanza

Z AMBIA'S RELATIONSHIP with the World Bank and the IMF goes back to 1956 and 1965, respectively. However, this long-standing relationship has not been without problems. The major aim of this paper is to provide a critical overview of the performance of the Zambian economy in light of the Bank's and the IMF's financial assistance, along with some thoughts on challenges of reform. The overview will focus mainly on the period following the resumption of Zambia's relationship with the two institutions, which had been severed between 1987 and 1989.

History of Zambia's Adjustment Programs

The Bank and the IMF argue that the imbalances that Zambia started to experience in the mid-1970s, apart from being direct consequences

The author expresses his gratitude to Denny Kalyalya for assisting in research and preparatory work for this paper.

[1]See, for example, Lionel Demery, "Structural Adjustment: Its Origins, Rationale, and Achievements," in *From Adjustment to Development in Africa: Conflict, Controversy, Convergence, Consensus?* ed. by Giovanni Andrea Cornia and Gerald K. Helleiner (New York: St. Martin's Press, 1994), pp. 25–48; Gerald K. Helleiner, "From Adjustment to Development in Sub-Saharan Africa: Consensus and Continuing Conflict," pp. 3–24 in the same book; Michael Roth, "Structural Adjustment in Perspective: Challenges for the 1990s," in *Democratization and Structural Adjustment in Africa in the 1990s*, ed. by Lual Deng, Markus Kostner, and Crawford Young (Madison, Wisconsin: African Studies Program, University of Wisconsin-Madison, 1991).

of the ensuing shocks, were due to inappropriate policies.[1] Over-expansionary fiscal and monetary policies, in conjunction with narrow tax bases and poor public enterprise performance, domestic pricing policies biased against agriculture, and overvalued currencies, are some of the policies cited. To correct these imbalances and face up to the challenges of restoring short-term internal and external equilibria and long-term economic development, the Bank and the IMF have urged countries to embark on economic reforms. The IMF-supported stabilization and Bank-supported adjustment programs, irrespective of the country of application, generally comprise two main objectives: macroeconomic stabilization and structural reforms.

What has been Zambia's experience with these adjustment programs? Unlike many other former colonies, Zambia inherited a relatively healthy economy at its independence in 1964.[2] This prosperity was directly linked to the booming copper industry. Thus, during the first decade after independence when copper prices were rising and domestic production of copper was increasing, the economy was able to grow at an average of 2.5 percent per annum. However, the first oil shock of 1973, the subsequent decline in copper prices (particularly since 1975), a general deterioration in the country's terms of trade, and the government's inability to develop a dynamic, diversified economy all combined to cause overall economic decline.

As a result, in 1973, Zambia adopted its first IMF-supported stabilization package. A total of SDR 19 million was extended to stem the decline in reserves and correct the budget deficit. But a continuing decline in the balance of payments compelled Zambia to enter into a second stand-by arrangement with the IMF in 1976 amounting to SDR 62 million, which involved imposing ceilings on the money supply, overall credit, and especially government credit. In addition, for the first time in the country's history, a devaluation of its currency, amounting to 20 percent, had to be effected. However, with the closure of the Southern Route,[3] due to an intensified war of liberation in Zimbabwe, the program did not yield any significant positive results.

In 1978, Zambia turned to the IMF again for a stand-by arrangement of SDR 317 million. Conditions for this facility included further restrictions on credit expansion and a 10 percent devaluation of the

---

[2]Zambia is a landlocked country, with an estimated population of 9.2 million inhabitants. Nearly 60 percent of the population is concentrated in four provinces (Southern, Central, Lusaka, and Copperbelt), along what is traditionally referred to as "the line of rail." The majority of the population lives on agriculture, which accounted for 18 percent of GDP, in real terms, in 1994.

[3]This is the rail route through Zimbabwe.

kwacha. However, in spite of the country having met all the conditions and the facility being totally disbursed, a further decline in copper prices and adverse weather conditions necessitated additional assistance. This time, the country went for an arrangement under the extended fund facility (EFF), amounting to SDR 800 million, covering 1981–83. Unlike the first three programs, which were directed at demand management, the EFF arrangement focused primarily on the supply side, namely, promotion of agriculture, mining, and manufacturing. Part of the explanation for this policy change was the tying of the loan to a three-year World Bank investment reorientation program, which was aimed at switching the focus from infrastructure to agricultural and industrial projects.

But by July 1982, Zambia had accumulated payment arrears and overshot the credit ceilings, and its balance of payments deficit had soared, forcing a cancellation of the EFF arrangement. Fortunately for Zambia, however, no sooner had this arrangement been canceled than the country entered into a fourth stand-by arrangement of SDR 270 million in 1983. Conditions for restoring internal balance included ceilings on money supply and credit, reducing the government's budget deficit to 5.6 percent of GDP, decontrol of prices of most goods, and a wage freeze. As for the external balance, a 20 percent devaluation was effected immediately, followed by a free float of the kwacha. The free float was soon replaced by a crawling peg of the kwacha to a basket of currencies deemed to reflect the major trading partners.

In spite of the above measures, however, the economy continued to falter. As a result, negotiations for yet another stand-by arrangement of SDR 225 million for the period 1984–86 were initiated and successfully concluded. This facility retained most of the measures of its predecessor, but also introduced the system of auctioning foreign exchange (beginning in October 1985)—perhaps the most controversial of the Bank-Fund-supported measures yet. Among other things, disbursement of the donor foreign exchange pledges necessary to sustain the system became erratic. The ensuing political discontent culminated in December 1986 in food riots on the Copperbelt and loss of life. Against this background, the government unilaterally abandoned the Bank-Fund-supported structural adjustment program in May 1987 and introduced its own New Economic Recovery Program (NERP87).

Upon adoption of NERP87 the Bank suspended loan disbursements to Zambia, which covered over 55 loans and credits, with total commitments in excess of $1 billion. Areas covered by these commitments included energy, transport and communications, rural water supply, education (secondary, higher, teacher training, and technical), commercial and small-holder agriculture, industrial forestry, and fisheries. NERP87 had as its theme "growth from our own resources." Its main elements included limiting debt service to 10 percent of net foreign exchange earnings, fixing the exchange rate at US$1 to K 8, reintroducing administrative allocation of foreign exchange through the Foreign Exchange Management and Allocation Committee, reintroducing price controls, and a continuous reviewing of policy. But by late 1988, Zambia was facing a rapidly deteriorating fiscal position, inflation was rising, foreign exchange shortages had become chronic, and black market activities were rampant. Severe difficulties were also encountered in servicing the external debt, much of which had been contracted on commercial terms.

Thus, in mid-1989, Zambia embarked on a Fund-Bank-supported (technically[4]) economic adjustment program aimed at creating a diversified and market-oriented economy. Recognizing the enormous external assistance required, Zambia had to negotiate for resumption of normal relations with its external creditors, which had been severed in the last decade. In July 1990, Zambia's economic and financial program was endorsed as a Fund-monitored program. Nine months later, in April 1991, the Fund approved a rights accumulation program, up to a maximum of SDR 836.9 million (the level of arrears to the Fund as of July 1, 1990), for the period 1991–94. However, policies went substantially off track in the second half of 1991 resulting in no rights accumulation. The new government (as of November 1991) then worked very hard to bring the program back on track. By the end of January 1992, Zambia had cleared its arrears to the Bank and reduced its arrears to the IMF to the end-1991 level. As a result, disbursements resumed in late 1992. On December 4, 1995, Zambia successfully completed its rights accumulation program and was granted a three-year arrangement under the enhanced structural adjustment facility (ESAF) and a one-year arrangement under the structural adjustment facility (SAF), totaling SDR 883.4 million, covering the period July 1995 to June 1998.

Recent Economic Performance

Clearly, Zambia has been experiencing serious economic difficulties since the first oil shock and collapse of world copper prices in the mid-1970s. Early efforts to restructure the economy proved inadequate. Moreover, the import substitution industrialization strategy that the government of the day adopted in an effort to accelerate growth of the

---

[4]Given Zambia's ineligibility for IMF or World Bank financial support.

manufacturing sector turned out to be very costly. The state became too entrenched in the running of most economic activities, and the types of industries that emerged were import using rather than import substituting. In the face of declining foreign exchange earnings due to the poor performance of the copper industry, capacity underutilization became the order of the day, leading to shortages of essential commodities and consequently inflation. Afraid that the situation would get out of hand—and in line with the adopted philosophy of Humanism—the state resorted to administrative controls of prices and allocation of resources. Overtime, these also bred their own problems, such as further capacity underutilization, long queues, and corruption.

In 1991, Zambians went to the polls and voted overwhelmingly to change the government. The new government has shown greater resolve to embrace structural adjustment programs, à la the IMF and the Bank. For instance, by 1992 a number of price controls were lifted, the Zambia Privatization Agency was created, the official and market exchange rates were unified, and nearly all subsidies were removed. In 1993, there was a further tightening of monetary policy, mainly to deal with escalating inflation, and a weekly treasury bill tender system was introduced.

By 1994, with the suspension of the Foreign Exchange Act, all forms of controls had been lifted. However, trade liberalization opened a floodgate to all sorts of imports, among them second-hand clothing (*Salaula*). One notable thing about *Salaula* is that it led to the demise of many of the local textile industries that had no competitive edge. This prompted the Zambia Association of Chambers of Commerce and Industry to cry "foul." Its members not only detested the influx of *Salaula* but also protested that some of the imports flooding the Zambian market were being dumped. The government responded by introducing countervailing duties in the 1994 budget, although due to the cumbersome procedure of invoking them, the duties have never really been applied. Thus, in 1995, the government introduced simpler measures to administer, including suspension of duty on a number of imported raw materials and a value-added tax (VAT). By 1995, the Zambian economy had, de facto, become a market economy *par excellence*.

Real Output Growth

Since the mid-1970s, Zambia has been experiencing protracted economic stagnation. Over the period 1985–93, while real GDP grew at an average of approximately 1.3 percent per year, the rate of population growth was estimated to have grown at an annual average of 3.2 percent—translating into a decline in GDP per capita of on average 4.6 percent annually. However, after four consecutive years of negative growth, a dramatic increase in real GDP of 6.5 percent was recorded in 1993. Unfortunately, this proved to be very short lived. Real GDP declined by 3.1 percent and 3.9 percent in 1994 and 1995, respectively—largely due to a fall in agricultural, forestry, and fishing sector outputs, resulting from drought, late delivery of inputs, and the high cost of credit.

Financial Sector Reforms

The financial sector has been one of the fastest-growing sectors since liberalization of the economy began. In 1994, even when the major productive sectors registered declines, the financial sector recorded the highest growth—13.8 percent. Over the course of 1994, 23 commercial banks were registered, with 18 of them operational. Also, by 1994, there were 43 *Bureaux de Change* and 30 nonbank financial institutions operating. As a result, competition became rife. By 1995, three banks had succumbed and had to be placed under receivership. Other notable developments in recent years included the revision of legislation relating to banking and financial services, and the establishment of a capital market.

The enactment of the Banking and Financial Services Act in 1994 is, among other things, aimed at empowering the Bank of Zambia as a lender of last resort and the bankers' bank. However, the failure of the aforementioned banks put this piece of legislation to a test. It became quite apparent that the central bank's presumed relative autonomy was yet to emerge.

With regard to the establishment of a capital market, Zambia's dream of a stock exchange became a reality on February 21, 1994, with the launching of the Lusaka Stock Exchange. Trading began in March 1994, and although business at first was slow, by mid-August over 2 million shares had been traded. Even so, the newness of the concept and continued prominence of commercial banks in providing business finance appear to be among the major factors retarding growth of the market.

Monetary and Credit Policies

The introduction of a weekly treasury bill tender system in January 1993—particularly the addition of 28-day bills to the menu of instruments in March—saw a dramatic increase in interest rates, which had been rising since the beginning of the year when they were decontrolled. The maximum lending rate for commercial banks rose from 85 percent in January 1993 to a peak of 139.3 percent in August 1993. Over the same period the savings rates increased from 51.28 percent to 97.9 percent, and the yield rate on 28-day treasury bills rose to 179.61

percent in August 1993 from 106 percent in March 1993. As expected, the increase in interest rates acted as a double-edged sword. On the one hand, it encouraged savings, but on the other hand, it discouraged investment.

The sale of treasury bills, of course, had fiscal repercussions, with the rise in treasury bill interest rates leading to an increase in national debt. By the end of 1994, national domestic debt had risen from a little over K 40 billion ($104 million) in January 1993 to K 150 billion ($220 million). It peaked at K 247 billion ($265 million) in October 1995, before falling to K 209 billion ($174 million) in March 1996. Such a huge domestic debt means that the government has to come up with more funds when retiring future national debt than would otherwise have been the case. Moreover, the persistently high domestic debt has been a major factor in the sluggish reduction in domestic interest rates and ultimately in inflation. Even so, it should be noted that nominal interest rates have now come down to the 50 percent level—relatively modest in real terms.

Further, the treasury bill tender system appears to have had another effect on the economy. Given the limited nature of Zambia's financial market and hence its financial base, the system reoriented demand away from the foreign exchange market. A cursory look at the financial market indicates that the treasury bill and foreign exchange markets are not mutually exclusive—they are both patronized by the same economic agents. Thus, it is not by sheer coincidence that as the treasury bill market prospered the kwacha appreciated.

Inflation

The government's commitment to reducing inflation, as announced in the 1992 budget, was reaffirmed in 1993 when the government declared inflation the "number one enemy" and vowed to observe "principles of sound finance." Major measures proposed included achieving a balanced budget, completely avoiding borrowing from the central bank, operating the government on a cash basis, and tightening the squeeze on excess bank reserves. These measures were to be complemented by sound exchange and interest rates policies.

Although inflation declined in 1993, it was still very high, averaging 187.1 percent for the year. Factors that contributed to this outturn were

---

[5]The government, under pressure from the public sector unions, awarded unbudgeted across-the-board salary increases of 50 percent.

[6]In 1992, Zambia and other Southern African countries experienced one of the severest droughts in recent history.

price instability during the first half of the year due to liquidity injection spillovers from 1992 public sector wage increases[5] and drought relief activities;[6] pricing policy changes in petroleum products and electricity; seasonal price changes in agricultural crops and products, particularly maize and its by-products; and persistent depreciation of the kwacha, which raised the prices of imported commodities and the cost of production given the country's high import dependence.

On the other hand, the drop in inflation experienced during the second half of 1993 came mainly from the Bank of Zambia's tough stance on money creation and the government's operation of a cash-based budget. These measures, in turn, contributed to the appreciation of the kwacha, which for the first time in a long time, led to a reduction in prices of some goods and services—particularly those directly related to exchange rate movements. The tough monetary and fiscal stance adopted in 1993 has continued in subsequent years. Consequently, the inflationary situation has generally been better than in the recent past—with inflation now down to an annualized 31 percent (end-November 1996).

Exchange Rate Policy

For policymakers, one of the major challenges has been exchange rate stability—and in that regard, Zambia has pursued virtually all types of exchange rate regimes (see Table 1).

Starting in the 1970s, the type of import substitution industrialization strategy that Zambia pursued made the economy extremely sensitive to

Table 1. Zambia's Exchange Rate Regimes

Period	Policy
1964–1971	Rate fixed to the pound sterling
1971: Q4–1976: Q2	Rate fixed to the U.S. dollar
1976: Q3–1983: Q3	July, pegged to the SDR with occasional devaluations
1983: Q3–1985: Q3	July, SDR link substituted by a crawling peg on a basket of currencies of trade partners
1985: Q4–1987: Q2	Foreign exchange auction; Dutch auction; two-tier auction
1987: Q3–1989: Q4	May, fixed rate, initially to the U.S. dollar and since Nov. 1988 to the SDR, with occasional devaluations
1990: Q1–1991: Q3	February 1990, dual exchange rate system with frequent small devaluations
1991: Q4–1992: Q3	April 1991, two windows unified; crawling peg continued
1992: Q4–1992: Q4	October 1992, *Bureau de Change*, two windows
1992: Q4–1993: Q4	December, two windows unified; flexible exchange rate system
1994: Q1–	Free market exchange rate; Exchange Control Act suspended

Source: World Bank, *Industrial Reorientation Project*, No. 10846, Attachment 10 (updated) (Washington: World Bank, 1992), p. 86; and Zambia, Ministry of Finance.

changes in the supply of foreign exchange. In a bid to rationalize the supply of foreign exchange, the government resorted to administrative allocation mechanisms that led to overvaluation of the exchange rate, foreign exchange shortages, and, ultimately, overheating of the economy. Initial attempts at liberalization and realignment of the exchange rate through devaluation only helped to instigate a stagflationary situation.

The new government that took office in November 1991 began a sustained liberalization of the exchange rate system and pursued a flexible exchange rate policy. An important step was the introduction of the *Bureau de Change* system in October 1992. Initially, the *Bureau de Change* system was to cater for small business transactions, as only earnings from nontraditional exports were channeled through the system. The bulk of the transactions were to be channeled through the Bank of Zambia under the Open General License system, established in 1990. This meant, de facto, that there were two foreign exchange windows—the *Bureau* window, where the exchange rate was supposed to be market determined and the Bank of Zambia window, where an official exchange rate reigned. Two months later, the two windows were unified and a flexible exchange rate system was adopted. Most of the remaining impediments to establishment of a free foreign exchange market were removed in January 1994 when the Exchange Control Act was suspended, and on November 30, 1994, the Open General License system was discontinued.

However, the fully liberalized foreign exchange market was received, especially at the beginning, with mixed feelings. On the one hand, people were excited about their newfound freedom in carrying out foreign exchange transactions openly and with ease. On the other hand, two major concerns were raised. First, there were fears that indiscriminate liberalization of the market, especially when the neighboring countries were still restrictive, would stimulate and accelerate capital flight.[7] Second, the relatively small growth in Zambia's exports has continued to raise doubts about the stability and hence sustainability of the system. The mining industry, the country's main source of foreign earnings, has been fraught with operational problems. Under these circumstances, donor inflows would have been the alternative source of foreign exchange. However, lately, this too has become precarious. As a result, the behavior of the kwacha/U.S. dollar exchange rate has become quite unstable (see Table 2).

---

[7]Information to prove or disprove this remains scanty.

Table 2. Kwacha/U.S. Dollar Exchange Rate
(End of period)

Year	Bank of Zambia Base Rate	Banks' Bureau Rates
1991	66.45	66.45
1992	184.21	180.27
1993	647.38	667.70
1994	680.81	703.37
1995	950.52	937.96
1996		
Jan.	977.18	995.97
Feb.	1,098.64	1,116.08
Mar.	1,201.40	1,224.37
Dec.	1,270.00	1,291.00

Source: Zambia, Ministry of Finance.

External Debt Service

Zambia continues to face serious balance of payments problems owing to three major factors: the country is too dependent on copper exports for its foreign exchange earnings (over 80 percent); the economy is highly import dependent, making it hypersensitive to fluctuations in the foreign exchange market; and the country has to contend with a huge external debt service burden.

Although Zambia's external debt has declined from its peak of $7.1 billion in 1992 to its current (end-1996) level of $6.2 billion, the situation is of great concern to the government and country as a whole (see Table 3). External debt as a proportion of GDP stands in the neighborhood of 200 percent—and given that export earnings are far less than GDP, this shows a serious lack of capacity to repay the debt. To illustrate, in 1991, external debt-service payments, excluding arrears, were equal to about 60 percent of the country's exports while external debt amounted to 560 percent of the exports of goods and services. In 1995, debt service totaled 328.9 million compared to the 1994 debt-service position of $301.8 million. Zambia's huge debt also has implications for resource allocation. Debt repayment diverts resources away from domestic development activities, which further erodes the country's capacity to repay the loans.

Resolution of the external debt situation has yet other complications, which arise mainly from the various interconnections among debt, exchange rates, and interest rates. For instance, although devaluation is aimed at increasing international competitiveness, it increases the local currency value of external liabilities and the budgetary costs of servicing the external debt. Variable interest rates, upon which most of the debt contracts are based, also add to the cost of repayment when they increase.

Table 3. Zambia's Total External Debt
(In billions of U.S. dollars)

1990	1991	1992	1993	1994	1995	1996
4.668	4.340	7.070	6.835	6.499	6.400	6.200

Sources: Bank of Zambia; Zambia, Ministry of Finance; and Zambia, National Commission for Development Planning.

In addition, such a large debt burden has the potential to lead to undue donor influence on macroeconomic policy. Zambia's foreign exchange earnings from copper exports are estimated at about $1 billion annually, whereas nontraditional exports, though increasing, are still substantially low with respect to the country's foreign exchange requirements. Thus, the donor community has been—and still is—a major source of foreign exchange, providing about $900 million annually. Unfortunately, donors impose conditions on both the source and use of those imports and link the support to macroeconomic policy performance. Lately, there have been shortfalls in donor balance of payments support, with serious repercussions on net international reserves, net claims on government, and net domestic assets benchmarks. This has arisen mainly because of donors invoking some of the conditionality clauses.

Fiscal Policy Developments

After many years of running fiscal deficits Zambia registered a fiscal surplus in 1993, although the surplus was, apparently, achieved at the expense of postponing certain payments—making the surplus, as some analysts have pointed out, a "suppressive surplus."[8]

However, it is fair to say that the government also took some stringent fiscal measures to stem the hitherto omnipresent deficits. These measures, which date back to the 1992 fiscal year, were augmented in 1993 when the government adopted a cash-based budget. The aim was to ensure that the primary balance was maintained throughout the fiscal year. This called for backing all intended expenditures with revenue. The cash budget and a zero balance on a cash basis at the end of the year has continued to be the major guiding principle for fiscal policy. To this end, the preliminary budgetary outturn for 1995 indicates a surplus of K 3.9 billion on the overall balance on a cash basis.

Even so, the government has had to face a number of difficulties, with some slippages that threatened macroeconomic stability. Fiscal slippage

---

[8]For instance, the government—afraid of fueling inflation and having decided to liberalize crop marketing, but faced with a poor private sector response—decided to issue promissory notes to farmers for their produce.

was largely caused early in 1995 by the government's attempt to bail out the ailing Meridien BIAO Bank, and later in the year by its commitment to pay depositors of the liquidated Meridien BIAO Bank and the other two banks under receivership (Commerce Bank and African Commercial Bank). There was also a lot of pressure on the budget, given the need to settle domestic arrears amounting to K 11.5 billion. Finally, revenue collections continued to fall short of expenditure, posing difficulties to manage the cash budget on a daily basis. This prompted the government to move away from the daily cash budget setup to a monthly cash budget, whose key feature was bridge financing from the Bank of Zambia. The goal was to facilitate the planning and orderly release of budgetary funding to line ministries and provinces.

On the *revenue* side, the increase in total domestic revenue during 1995 can be attributed to government efforts to step up revenue collection in order to meet growing expenditure. New tax measures included the introduction of the VAT (pegged at 20 percent across the board), the imposition of a 5 percent import declaration fee, and the increase in taxes on some goods and services. The government also stepped up tax administration and enforcement measures.

On the *expenditure* side, the government has made expenditure reduction the main focus of its fiscal reform. Noninterest expenditure as a percentage of GDP was to be reduced from 16 percent in 1991 to 14 percent in 1992. However, for a variety of reasons, including drought relief, this target could not be met. Instead, actual expenditure rose to 31 percent of GDP and, unfortunately, this trend of actual expenditure exceeding budgeted expenditure has continued.

Agriculture

Agriculture has long been recognized as the area offering immediate and great potential for diversification and sustainable economic and social development. This stems from the observation that Zambia has a total land area of 75 million hectares, out of which about 24 million hectares is arable land (i.e., suitable for agriculture production). However, out of these 24 million, only about 2 million are under cultivation annually and slightly over 10 million are used for grazing. Under normal circumstances the country receives adequate rainfall that can support a variety of rainfed crops, and approximately 45 percent of the fresh water resources in the Southern African subregion are found in Zambia.[9]

---

[9]See C. Mab-Zeno, C. Mudenda, and others, *Zambia: Natural Resource Study* (Washington: World Bank, 1993).

However, the agriculture sector's performance has remained below its full potential.[10] During the 1994/95 crop season, a prolonged drought resulted in large declines in yields of most crops—exacerbated by an inadequate supply of inputs, the high cost of credit, and poor marketing arrangements. Agriculture, forestry, and fishing production declined further by 11.3 percent that season. The substantial decline in food crops output resulted in a grain shortage, prompting the need for imports. The government turned to donors for assistance in the form of commodity aid to meet part of the shortfall.

Reasons for unrealized potential include excessive government intervention and control of markets (during the reign of the previous government), and inadequate provision of essential public services. Marketing of most commodities was for a long time a preserve of either parastatals or government-appointed agents. In an effort to eliminate some of these excesses, the government embarked on agricultural reform, making the sector as a whole the "project"—the first time Zambia had tried the sector-based approach—to ensure better coordination and efficient resource allocation.

The Agricultural Sector Investment Program is a four to five year program. The proposed strategies include liberalization of markets with the government playing only an indirect and supportive role, crop diversification to facilitate appropriate crop rotation, development of the livestock subsector, emphasis on the provision of services to smallholder producers, better provision of infrastructure, improved access to inputs and markets for outlying regions, improvement of the economic status of women (through restructuring of agricultural research, extension, credit, and land tenure policies), judicious and full utilization of land suitable for agriculture, assisting farmers to deal with natural disasters, and placing the emphasis on sustainable agriculture.

Industry

From independence through the early 1980s, Zambia's industrialization strategy revolved around state ownership and direction of important industrial enterprises, major public investments in intermediate sectors (e.g., chemicals, fertilizers, and cement) and consumer durables (e.g., automobile assembly), restriction of foreign competition through import licensing and tariffs, and promotion of import substitution industrialization through high levels of protection, investment controls, restrictive licensing, and other regulatory devices. The resources for the

---

[10]See Zambia, Ministry of Agriculture, Food, and Fisheries, *A Framework for Agricultural Policies to the Year 2000 and Beyond* (Lusaka: MAFF, 1992).

strategy were expected to come from the mining industry's foreign exchange earnings and tax revenues.

However, Zambia's industrial growth has not been very impressive. The index of industrial production (with 1980 as base year) has been negative, dropping to −7.6 percent in 1991. Capital expenditure as a percentage of GDP (in constant 1977 prices) has remained very small (about 3 percent) and has generally been declining. Similarly, gross fixed capital formation (in constant 1977 prices) continues to be a small proportion of GDP, ranging from 5.5 percent to 10.3 percent over the period 1987 to 1992. In short, the industrial sector is characterized by low capacity utilization, declining labor productivity, high capital intensity, and import dependence—in the past compounded by critical foreign exchange shortages. In 1995, real output in this sector declined by 4.5 percent, largely due to low capacity utilization of plants and machinery, which averaged 25 percent.

The poor performance notwithstanding, the previous and present governments have long recognized the importance of the industrial sector, as exemplified by the Industrial Development Act (1977) and Investment Acts (1986 and 1991). The 1991 Act sets strict ground rules on expropriations and other forms of government intervention in investment decisions, provides guarantees against nationalization of foreign-owned enterprises, and provides for the establishment of the Investment Centre (which promotes, coordinates, and monitors investments, as well as serving as a one-stop support facility to investors).

Parastatals and Privatization

Although Zambia had a very prosperous economy at independence, control and direction were concentrated in foreign private hands. This prompted the state to nationalize what it termed the "commanding heights" of the economy. By the 1990s, about 80 percent of industrial and commercial activities were controlled by the parastatal sector. Over 150 parastatals had been established—ranging in size from the giant mining company (the Zambia Consolidated Copper Mines) to breweries and small bakeries.

However, state-owned enterprises often had to contend with conflicting social and commercial objectives. At the insistence and directive of the government, many companies had to sell their goods at below-market prices, subsidize the public—particularly urban workers and dwellers—and employ more workers than needed to ameliorate unemployment. In addition, decision making tended to be overcentralized. This, coupled with a bureaucratization of management, led to the emergence of inefficient companies that could not perform.

In response, in 1992, the government embarked on a rigorous privatization exercise to scale down the government's direct initiative in economic activities and administrative load; reduce government budgetary costs arising from subsidies and capital expenditure; promote competition and improve the efficiency of enterprise operations; encourage wide ownership of shares; promote the growth of capital markets; stimulate local and foreign investment; and raise capital income for the treasury. By November 1994, 14 state-owned enterprises had been privatized, and by December, the program had realized more than K 15 billion. The program gained momentum in 1995 when a total of 30 companies were privatized through management buyouts and public flotation on the Lusaka Stock Exchange.

Social Impact of Adjustment

As is well known, structural adjustment implies fundamental changes in the structure of the economy and in the welfare of the people. However, as the process unravels, certain sections of the population are likely to bear more than their share of the burden of adjustment. Recently, opposition political parties and the Labour Movement have criticized adjustment programs precisely on this point.

Equity and sustainable development demand that the vulnerable in society be protected. Until fairly recently, however, very little attention—let alone resources—was directed toward this goal. It is disheartening to note that most of the resources to ameliorate the impact of social adjustment have come from or been initiated by donors.[11]

Health

Until the change of government in 1991, Zambia was characterized by free universal health care. This had to change, as the health care system had virtually collapsed. There were acute shortages of drugs and medical supplies; the health infrastructure was in a state of disrepair; and morale of the health providers was at an all-time low owing to poor remuneration and working conditions. As a result, there was an exodus of medical doctors, with the number of doctors dropping from 621 in 1991 to 537 in 1992.

In 1992, the new government embarked on restructuring the health sector. The program is based on the principle that every able-bodied

---

[11]See D.H. Kalyalya and G.N. Muuka, "Structural Adjustment, Macroeconomic Demand Management, Food Policy Reform and Its Impact on Rural and Urban Poverty in Zambia: Lessons, Prospects, and Options," paper presented to a regional seminar on Integration of Poverty Alleviation Strategies into Economic Policies, Malawi, Blantyre, July 11–21, 1994.

person residing in Zambia and earning an income should contribute toward the maintenance of their health, with an emphasis on primary health care. Additional measures, including introduction of medical fees and legislation to allow the establishment of private clinics and hospitals, were introduced in 1993. The quest for improving health care services is ongoing. In nominal terms, government allocations to the health sector have been increasing from 8 percent in 1993 to 14.3 percent in 1996.

Education

The education sector—with an adult illiteracy rate of over 30 percent—has experienced similar problems to those observed in the health sector: dilapidated physical infrastructure; lack of equipment; shortage of qualified teachers; poor conditions of service, and hence low morale with a staff exodus; high teacher-student ratios; and donor dependence.

The government's major reform objectives include providing every eligible child with a good quality education, universal primary education, and carrying out and maintaining quantitative and qualitative improvements in tertiary education. To this end, in 1992, the government vowed to rehabilitate and maintain institutions of learning; provide learning materials, school desks, and equipment; and expand primary schools ending at Grade 4 to upper primary schools, particularly in rural areas.

Progress, however, has proved to be slow and highly demanding in resource terms, prompting the government to introduce additional measures in 1993. These included decentralization, encouragement of community and private sector participation in providing education services, and establishment of a subcommittee of the national Social Sector Rehabilitation and Maintenance Task Force. Other measures raised the nominal allocation to education from 9.8 percent to 13 percent of total government expenditure, and included cost-recovery and cost-sharing schemes at all learning institutions. The latter took the form of user charges levied by Parent-Teacher Associations, boarding fees at secondary schools, and loans to university students.

In 1994, a further impetus was given to decentralization as district education management boards and school management boards were asked to take full responsibility for teachers, pupils, education infrastructure, school furniture, and learning materials. Only functions such as policy formulation, curriculum development, standard settings, and evaluation were to be performed at the ministry headquarters. Accordingly, the government increased the budgetary allocation to the ministry from 13 percent to 15 percent of the total national budget, and in 1995, the allocation went up to 19 percent.

Employment and Unemployment

The first few years following Zambia's political independence were marked by rapid increases in formal sector employment—jumping some 46.1 percent between 1964 and 1975. The rapid rise was basically due to highly favorable foreign exchange earnings from copper exports, which enabled the country to embark upon a number of public capital projects that helped create jobs.

However, as the balance of payments situation deteriorated in the mid-1970s, employment opportunities began to dwindle. The economy's inability to cope with the level of imports was accompanied by excess plant capacities, in turn leading to reduced demand for formal sector employment. The situation was made worse by rapid population growth and, by extension, rapid labor force growth. Thus, the government's plans to increase formal sector employment by 20,000 persons annually from 1980–84 could not be realized. During that period, the labor force grew at 3.8 percent a year while the economy was merely growing at 0.2 percent a year.

The poor economic performance of the 1980s, unfortunately, has continued in the 1990s. Making matters worse, the labor force has continued to grow at a fast rate—about 4 percent annually. Current economic reforms, before yielding intended results, are likely to add to the pool of the unemployed. Already, in the first half of 1994 a total of 3,669 workers were declared redundant.

Reflections on Economic Reform

What are the lessons for reform? First, it appears that *stabilization measures are easier to implement than structural adjustment measures.* This stems from the observation that the latter requires striking and maintaining a careful balance between tight and expansionary monetary and fiscal policies. Moreover, during the stabilization phase, a number of problems—including unemployment and an output squeeze from high interest rates—are apt to get worse. Thus, poverty alleviation measures need to be instituted simultaneously to take care of those segments of society who are likely to fall through the cracks of adjustment, as it were. This, I am afraid, seems to be quite an elusive objective.

Second, it is important to recognize that *while inappropriate policies invariably result in poor economic performance, good policies can do little more than permit, or at most, encourage an improved economic performance.* Economic reform is not only about "getting prices right"—such as a favorable exchange rate, positive real interest rates, appropriate incentives for farmers, a sustained fiscal balance, and a positive external trade picture—it is also about establishing an institutional framework to support "correct" policies.

Third, it is important to realize that *in Zambia the reform process faces other complications:*

• The economy's structure, with its heavy dependence on copper, makes short-term gains in the mining sector from economic reform extremely difficult, thus serving as a brake on economic growth for the economy as a whole.

• With close to 50 percent of the population living in urban areas, Zambia is one of the most urbanized countries in sub-Saharan Africa. This dictates that the social consequences of reform should be taken into account at an early stage of the program.

• Adopting a "big bang" approach to liberalization has its weaknesses and strengths. Policy sequencing, evaluation, and monitoring become quite complicated. On the other hand, hindsight knowledge seems to suggest that had the government waited to undertake some of the reforms, it most probably would not have had the courage to do so, given the population's impatience with awaiting the delivery of the goods.

Fourth, *there is an urgent need to seriously look into Zambia's debilitating debt.* Currently, Zambia's external debt stands at $6.4 billion, or about K 141 billion, in real terms. This works out to be about 65 times the size of the country's GDP. It also means that every Zambian owes the international community approximately $700, making Zambia the most indebted country in per capita terms. The foregoing amply demonstrates the country's inability now and in the foreseeable future to repay such a huge debt. And as long as this issue remains unresolved the country's development prospects will continue to be stifled.

Fifth, another issue impinging on Zambia's future prospects is economic management. *With sound economic management, a number of problems, particularly those relating to resource misallocation, could be tackled effectively.* For instance, the successes the country has scored in the last two years in dampening inflation and liberalization can be maintained only if there is good management. Similarly, the government's recently announced measures to stimulate industry will require judicious implementation. Unfortunately, we are in an election year, and electioneering might sway government efforts from development issues.

In conclusion, Zambia's prospects for economic recovery and sustainable development critically depend on sound economic management and external support. Moreover, there is a need for more deliberate actions geared toward accomplishing a clearly defined vision.

12

Improving Overseas Development Assistance: The Broad Sector Approach

Michael Foster

IN RECENT YEARS, donors have been developing sector-wide approaches to providing development assistance, as an alternative to traditional project aid. This new approach to development cooperation mainly derives from some ideas developed by Steve Denning in the Africa Department of the World Bank and is most fully described in a World Bank discussion paper by Peter Harrold and Associates.[1]

In my remarks today, I would like to talk first of all about the budget context for external aid and some of the problems with the traditional project approach that have led donors to think about sector-based approaches. I will also discuss some of the problems with reforming budget management, as a context and to some extent a prerequisite for sector aid. I will then go on to describe the main features of the sector approach—which is now a central element of the World Bank's lending strategy in Africa—with an example drawn from Zambia's health sector investment program. I will conclude with some comments on critical success factors for the sector approach and the role of conditionality in these programs.

---

[1]Peter Harrold and Associates, *The Broad Sector Approach to Investment Lending: Sector Investment Programs,* World Bank Discussion Paper No. 302 (Washington: World Bank, Africa Technical Department, 1995).

The Budget Context for Aid

Most official development assistance is channeled via the government budget. It is fungible, which means that donor funds spent on, for example, a health project may release a government's own resources to finance another activity entirely if the government substitutes the donor project funds for expenditure that it would otherwise have funded from its own resources. It is government budget decisions that determine how aid is used. This does not mean that more aid necessarily leads to more government spending. Governments have three main options for how they can use external assistance from donors: they can increase spending, reduce taxation, or reduce their borrowing. The last two options can provide direct benefits to the private sector (lower taxes, easier credit). Increased spending can also provide indirect benefits to the private sector, if it is used wisely to improve infrastructure and essential services.

African budgets and budget management have some characteristic weaknesses. These are not found everywhere in Africa, and many of these features are improving in many countries. Nevertheless, common weaknesses include:

- large deficits that strangle private access to credit;
- a low tax effort, often lacking fairness and transparency;
- too much spent on projects and salaries, too little on operation and maintenance;
- subsidies and spending priorities that are poorly targeted, often benefiting small minorities of the population;
- budgets that are fragmented by dependency on aid; and
- poor levels of accountability, with an ever-present risk of corruption.

These weaknesses mean that donors cannot be indifferent as to how aid resources are used in the economy. Certainly, a stronger domestic budget performance would help governments to use aid more productively. For this reason, donors have pressed governments to define a clear macroeconomic framework, with clear targets for the budget—including the roles of domestic and external finance, and the level and sectoral shares of spending.

Problems with Projects

In the aid-dependent countries of Africa, donors have themselves contributed significantly to the budget problems. One of the most important reasons for developing the sector approach has been an increasing recognition of the serious problems resulting from the project approach.

There is *too much project aid relative to resources for operation and maintenance,* with donors reluctant to pay directly for operation and maintenance. Donors do contribute indirectly through counterpart funds from balance of payments support, but there remains an imbalance between the resources available for project commitments and those available for nonsalary current costs.

There are *too many donor-driven projects,* making it impossible to develop and implement a coherent, consistent policy for the sector as a whole.

Local management capacity is undermined by the need to service donor projects. The proliferation of donors, of projects, and of visiting missions to discuss projects absorbs a disproportionate amount of the time of senior managers in African governments. Donor projects tend to absorb many of the best staff, while heavy use of expatriate advisers tends to reduce local ownership and inhibit the building of local skills and experience.

Donor projects may escape budget disciplines. Too many donors go directly to line ministries rather than going, as they should, to the ministries of finance and planning. Donors often fail to give sufficient reporting of commitments and disbursements on the projects that they are implementing. This lack of financial information makes it very difficult for the central economic ministries, or line ministries, to plan resource allocation in line with their priorities.

A project approach tends to lead to *inconsistent standards of provision* across the sector as a whole. Islands of excellence within project areas are surrounded by oceans of underprovision elsewhere. Where donor projects exist, they draw in most of the available funding and most of the management attention. Outside the areas where there happen to be projects, there is very little.

Efforts at Budget Management Reform

Governments and donors are trying to overcome some of these problems by moving away from a project approach toward general financial support to implement agreed sector policy and expenditure plans. But to make this possible at the sector level, it is also necessary to develop a framework of overall improvements in budget management. The Special Programme of Assistance to Africa (SPA) has been giving some attention to this and has produced draft guidelines that were recently discussed with African officials at a meeting in Malawi organized by the

German GTZ (Gesellschaft für Technische Zusammenarbeit). There are plans to hold similar discussions with Francophone countries. I should stress that the SPA donors are not trying to impose these guidelines without first fully discussing them with our African partners and taking their views into account.

What are the main features of these guidelines? First, governments should be asked to prepare medium-term budget frameworks, rolled forward annually, and to discuss the frameworks and their priorities with the donors. This does not mean that donors will try to dictate priorities, but they do have a legitimate need to be consulted. Donors need to be satisfied that the substantial donor flows are balanced by sufficient efforts to raise domestic resources, that they actually lead to additional development spending, and that spending priorities reflect development goals and an efficient balance between capital and the recurrent budgets.

Second, the guidelines ask governments to also prepare action plans for achieving acceptable standards of budget management and accountability. It is recognized that financial management systems are weak in many countries and that one cannot overcome those problems overnight. A coherent medium-term approach is needed. At present, efforts to improve financial management are often fragmented, driven by donor technical assistance, and with significant waste and duplication.

Third, the guidelines envisage that progress in implementing both the medium-term budget framework and the action plan for improving budget management should be monitored by governments, as well as reported on and discussed both with donors locally and at country Consultative Group meetings.

Finally, donors on their side also have a responsibility to respond to these efforts to improve the budget management process. Where governments embark upon a credible process of reform, donors should respond by only supporting programs and projects that are included within the budget framework, working toward channeling their assistance via the budget, and making use of the governments' own financial management procedures. The broad sector approach provides, in principle, a convenient instrument for doing this. Conversely, where the budget management is not being reformed, it will be difficult to introduce sector programs.

Main Features of the Broad Sector Approach

The main features of the broad sector approach are, first, that there should be a medium-term expenditure framework that determines the size of the resource envelope for the sector. It is essential that the re-

sources to be made available to the sector program from both government and donors are determined by careful consideration of overall national priorities.

Second, the government should lead a process for drawing up a comprehensive program for the sector and agreeing to it with the donors.
The program needs to set out clearly:

- the policy framework for the sector;
- objectives and performance measures over the period of the sector
  program;
- the institutional responsibilities for implementing the program, together with an assessment of capacity of relevant institutions and
  proposals for strengthening them as necessary;
- financial arrangements, covering budget preparation and agreement, arrangements for appraisal and approval of subprojects and
  components forming part of the strategy, procurement and disbursement procedures, and accounting and audit arrangements;
- management arrangements, including reporting and monitoring;
  and
- details of the expenditure program on both the capital and the recurrent side, including identifying the recurrent cost implications of
  the capital investment budget. In practice, the sector program is
  likely to require that a rolling budget be prepared, specified in de-
  tail for the current budget year, and rolled forward annually.

Another key feature of the approach is that all significant donors to
the sector should provide their support to the sector as part of the sector program, preferably using common procedures.

Zambia's Health Sector Investment Program

The Zambia Health Sector Investment Program was one of the first
of the broad sector programs to be established, and it is useful to compare it with the blueprint.

Zambia's sector investment program has a very clear policy framework in the form of the strategic health plan. There is strong leadership
and commitment to the plan at the political and official level. There is
a very clear focus on decentralization, with a bigger proportion of the
health sector budget going to support district health services rather than
supporting the central hospitals. All of the main donors are essentially
committed and supportive of the program.

However, there are a number of divergences from the blueprint. First,
there is no real medium-term expenditure framework for the health
sector. Zambia is struggling to restore macroeconomic stability to the

economy and is operating on an annual cash budget. This makes it extremely hard to judge the level of health services that can be sustained in the medium term. Moreover, there is no clear procedure for adjusting the sector program in the light of developments in the macroeconomy.

Common donor disbursement procedures are limited so far to district services, and even the support for district services is not fully integrated within the government budget. Donors are putting in resources through common procedures for part of the program, but not for the program as a whole. Some of that funding is in practice additional to the budget, and there is no clear procedure for adjusting donor commitments according to overall budget developments. As a consequence, there is a serious danger that the sector program may prevent rather than assist sound prioritization of the budget as a whole.

The World Bank has argued against significant use of long-term technical assistance in sector programs, on the grounds that this reduces ownership and prevents the building of local capacity. However, this is a somewhat controversial issue between the World Bank and the bilateral donors, with the bilateral donors more inclined to support the use of technical assistance, provided it is within a context of strong government leadership.

A number of steering committees have been established to implement the Zambia health program, with government and donor representation. Donors who are not locally represented have tended not to be represented on these committees—for example, the World Bank does not participate. It is not clear to what extent this has so far been a problem, but it may suggest that the level of monitoring needed by such complex programs is easier to achieve with strong representation in the field.

Key Factors for Success

What are the key success factors that emerge from the experience to date? First, *strong leadership from the government side,* including political commitment to tackle the key problems of the sector. This typically needs to encompass institutional reform, appropriate staffing levels and remuneration, and clear prioritization of resources. In the absence of leadership willing to grapple with these issues, or of a donor community willing to insist that they be addressed, the sector approach can end up perpetuating unsuccessful policies and approaches. In the absence of accompanying reforms, the approach could become little more than an instrument whereby the donors push heavier resources into their favorite sectors, typically health and education, leaving the country with bloated social sectors that are still spending resources inefficiently, unsustainably, and with little effect.

Second, *macroeconomic stability and predictable budgets* are fundamental to judging sustainability, and it is doubtful that sector programs should be attempted in their absence.

Third, securing *adequate commitment and motivation of those required to change their behavior* requires not only political leadership but may also need to be supported by an effective process of civil service reform and capacity building. In the Ghana civil service reform program, the intention is to prepare performance improvement programs for individual departments and ministries. Sequencing of this civil service reform program is intended to give early priority to those sectors that are going to be the subject of sector investment programs to ensure that problems of capacity and motivation are addressed.

Fourth, common disbursement arrangements are impossible unless donors have *confidence in the accounting arrangements*. It is probably realistic to proceed cautiously, adopting common disbursement arrangements on those parts of the program where accountability is reasonably strong and where costs can be saved. There are probably strong economies of scale for using common procedures to support local level services, and the Zambia health experience suggests that the accounting problems can be addressed successfully. At the other extreme, it may be rather less harmful to continue to rely upon donor expertise in major offshore procurement, especially where local capacity is lacking.

Fifth, the approach needs *donors' willingness to merge their efforts and accept lower visibility of their own funds*. This will be helped by establishing attractive and viable real world objectives. Donors will have less need to put their Union Jack or their Tricoleur on the side of a clinic or a school if they can say instead that their finance has contributed to a program that has raised national educational attainment or has reduced the infant mortality rate by some measurable amount.

Finally, we need to recognize that it takes a long time to put the sector programs together, and *donors should not force the pace* on the government or on other donors. If a donor arrives with a planeload of advisors for a three-week mission and expects to sign a loan at the end of it, there will not be much local ownership and it will not be a very soundly based program.

Role of Conditionality

The sector program approach is part of an evolving consensus on new approaches to conditionality. It is increasingly recognized that conditions are more likely to be complied with when the government agrees that the proposed action is necessary. Conditionality usually fails when conditions are imposed as a cost of obtaining a loan or grant. This is especially true when conditionality is applied to difficult institutional and management reforms of the type that are typical of the sector approach, and where meaningful conditions are also much more difficult to formulate.

There is a hierarchy of conditions. The *overall level of aid* to a country increasingly depends on a general assessment of governance and economic and social policies. At the *macroeconomic level,* balance of payments assistance is dependent on adherence to a reform program agreed with the Bretton Woods institutions. *Sectoral programs* come below this level. They are usually conditional upon implementing agreed sector policies and programs, but without explicit macroeconomic conditions. *Project aid* typically has only project-level conditions.

The level of commitments at each level within this hierarchy probably depends on conditions at the higher level being satisfied so that, for example, a new project commitment would not normally be entered into in the absence of a satisfactory sector policy. Sector program commitments may well depend on a macroeconomic framework being in place. However, once that commitment has been made, the implementation of a sector program ought to depend only on sector-level conditions. Support for a medium-term sector program ought not to be interrupted because the IMF program has gone off track, for example, unless one of the consequences has been that sector commitments are also not being met.

Sector programs should be thought of as being more concerned with partnership than conditionality. They should set out what all partners agree to do in order to develop the sector:
- agreed objectives;
- resources and who will provide them;
- institutional responsibility;
- the policy framework in which the program will operate;
- the procedure for monitoring and course correction; and
- the accounting and financial management arrangements.

All partners accept obligations: the government to implement the program, and donors to provide resources if the program is implemented as agreed. Both sides make commitments.

Conclusions

The traditional donor approach to aid, via balance of payments support and project aid, obscures how additional resources are actually used by governments. Donor resources are fungible, and overall budget management should become an increasingly important factor in allocating aid resources. Countries that set out attractive medium-term budget frameworks and make progress toward achieving good standards of budget management are well placed to mobilize donor support for their priority programs. In these circumstances, sector investment programs are a particularly appropriate instrument for donor support. However, great care is needed to ensure that the sector approach does not raise aid dependence. Domestic resource mobilization needs to increase over time in Africa to permit a rising share of donor resources to be used for development, not recurrent costs.

Comments

Peter Warutere

For the first time in a decade, the real income of individuals in sub-Saharan Africa is growing, mainly as a result of strong GDP growth, which was estimated at 3.5–4 percent in 1995. This is the highest growth the continent has achieved since 1990, according to a new World Bank report, *Global Economic Prospects and the Developing Countries*.[1] Prospects for higher growth appear much stronger than ever before.

In assessing this remarkable recovery of countries that have been ravaged by civil wars, drought, and weak economic and political systems, there are perhaps two critical factors that could be considered to have influenced this growth: some of the countries benefited from improvements in export commodity prices while others benefited from the strong structural reforms that they have adopted, or a combination of both. Indeed, more than 30 of the 48 African countries have achieved a growth of 3 percent or more and now show strong signs of sustainable long-term development. The opening up of South Africa, which has sustained recovery for two consecutive years, and the peace prevailing in the once war-torn Mozambique and Angola have strengthened growth in the Southern Africa region. Other economies in the region that have remained stable—notably, Botswana, Lesotho, and Zimbabwe—continue to exhibit reasonably high levels of growth.

In the East African region, Kenya, Tanzania, and Uganda are rapidly emerging as showcases of successful transformation through structural adjustment programs. Uganda has achieved a tremendous recovery from years of civil war, with an estimated growth rate of 10 percent in 1995, and Kenya's GDP rose an estimated 5.2 percent the same year—prospects for a faster growth rate of 6 percent appear more likely than ever before. For the first time, per capita GDP has started rising, after falling to $270 in 1993, which was the worst year in the history of Kenya, with GDP growth at a mere 0.2 percent. By the end of 1996, per capita GDP is projected to rise to $310.

However, Central and Western Africa still show a fair number of economies in serious distress, despite modest growth in countries such as Benin, Central African Republic, Côte d'Ivoire, Ghana, Guinea, and

---

[1]World Bank, *Global Economic Prospects and the Developing Countries* (Washington: World Bank, 1996).

156

Nigeria. Some of the other countries in the region, such as Cameroon, Congo, and Senegal, have just emerged from a period of negative growth but show promising signs of recovery, though troubled Zaïre still suffers from negative growth.

Structural Adjustment Programs

The success of structural adjustment programs is difficult to measure in isolation, considering the other factors that influence the growth and development of the sub-Saharan African countries. Even so, the reforms have admittedly contributed to growth in countries that have recently shown strong signs of recovery.

In Kenya, for instance, the success of structural reforms is best illustrated by its substantial recovery since 1993. Liberalization of trade and exchange rates, removal of price controls and interest rate guidelines, divestiture of state investment in commercial enterprises, monetary and fiscal policy reforms, and the removal of exchange controls have greatly improved business confidence, with the economy the strongest it has been in over five years. Inflation is down to less than 2 percent (from over 100 percent in June 1993), the money supply is under check, and national savings and domestic investment as a percentage of GDP have been restored to over 20 percent. Foreign exchange availability, which was a critical factor in determining growth before the liberalization started, is no longer depressing business growth. At one point in August 1993, the entire economy had only $80 million of foreign reserves, which was barely enough to cover three weeks of imports. Today, the foreign reserves held by both the central bank and commercial banks is in excess of $1 billion, equivalent to more than five months of import cover, and the exchange rate remains fairly stable. However, high interest rates, on average about 30 percent, have a negative impact on business growth and heavy government borrowing is a major source of concern.

Structural adjustment programs have also encouraged recovery in many other countries. By implementing reforms, these economies have had access to aid that has mainly been used for rehabilitating infrastructure and for balance of payments and economic stabilization programs. In most of the countries, export trade and tourism have improved thanks to a new sense of competitiveness. It is also important to note that economic integration—or increased regional trade where integration is not yet actualized—has played a significant role in the economic transformation of these countries. This is particularly evident in Southern Africa, Western Africa, and, more recently, Eastern Africa.

Conflicts in the Reform Process

Until recently, many of the African leaders, including those who have embraced reforms, were suspicious about the real motives of the donor-supported structural adjustment programs. They had reason to be, particularly when the donor nations tried to push economic reforms at the same time that they demanded political democratization. In many countries, Kenya included, reforms were taken as prescriptions that the donors were imposing to create fertile ground for political reforms. Indeed, the Western world used both economic and political reforms as preconditions for new aid support—creating a serious conflict, because the donor nations were seen to have found allies in opposition parties to use aid to press for political changes.

The source of conflict was primarily founded in the fear by incumbent leaders of losing both political and economic power. By adopting reforms, the leaders realized the danger of losing the powerful control that they maintained on economic and political systems. They could no longer, for instance, use officially controlled foreign exchange allocations to gain political support or use state enterprises to reward their political supporters. Reforms meant that these leaders would no longer have unlimited economic resources at their disposal to buy votes from the electorate and influence economic and political policy.

In addition, the structuring of adjustment programs caused resistance among leaders, who felt that the programs were prescribed by outsiders unfamiliar with the intricate domestic conditions. There was, for instance, concern that reforms were aggravating poverty and unemployment by increasing the cost of basic goods and services, reducing the workforce in the public sector, and exposing local enterprises to foreign competition. But the World Bank and the IMF have tried to show that the pains of reforms are short term, because sustained recovery will provide tremendous opportunities for increasing incomes and reducing poverty and unemployment.

In recent years, donors have recognized the need to mobilize popular support for reforms by involving governments and other interested parties in the design and discussion of structural reforms. In Kenya, for instance, the new Policy Framework Paper for 1996–98, designed by the government, in consultation with the IMF and World Bank staffs, has been widely publicized and discussed—this was the first time that there has been a public dialogue on the policy document. Through dialogue on both economic and political issues, governments and donors have learned to accommodate each other and work together. Hence, the greater acceptance of structural adjustment programs in Africa.

There is another important factor that appears to be influencing the pace of reforms in Africa. The donor nations seem to have changed their hostile stance against the governments in power, primarily because the donors have failed to develop a useful partnership with the opposition parties. The disappointing performance of the main opposition parties—Kenya is a good example of this—have forced the donors to shift their alliances. In any case, they have realized that by using hard prescriptions like withholding aid to countries that have not embraced reforms, they are simply intensifying the sufferings of the masses and encouraging the leaders to continue applying corrupt practices for survival. What the donors have come to appreciate is that their actions do not really hit their targets.

Furthermore, they do not want to be accused of engaging in personalized fights with particular leaders under the guise of pushing for reforms. This conflict has been seen in the way the donors have treated Kenya and Uganda, for example. Even after undertaking numerous economic reforms and allowing political opposition, Kenya's balance of payments aid—which was suspended in November 1991—was not fully restored until February 1996. However, Uganda continued to receive substantial donor support, despite publicly resisting political opposition. The same argument could be applied when considering the rather cozy relationship between the Western world and some countries with poor human rights records, notably China.

It is also important to note that, by easing their demands for aid disbursement, donors have put themselves in a difficult position with opposition parties and human rights groups in countries where economic and political concerns persist. This is perhaps aptly illustrated in Kenya, where political activists argue that the conditions for resumption of aid have still not been fulfilled, considering the official indifference to corruption, human rights abuses, and registration of new political parties. The conflict arises from the thin line between what has been achieved and what should, ideally, be the trigger point for aid. The donors and the government presumably look at the pace and progress of the reform process, while the government critics argue on the grounds of the promises that have yet to be fulfilled.

Agenda for Sustainable Development in Africa

While the success of structural adjustment programs in influencing Africa's political transformation is acknowledged, the future growth of African countries will depend on the benefits of more open market economies, economic integration, and greater opportunities in export trade and tourism. Structural reforms have to be deepened but the donors should use aid less as a condition for influencing structural reforms.

Africa no doubt needs massive aid injections, which is now likely with the $25 billion special initiative launched recently by the United Nations. Many countries will continue to rely on donor support to develop their vital infrastructure (roads, energy, water supply, health, and educational facilities) but will require less subventions to maintain their bloated public sector bureaucracies. However, there should be a sustained effort to reduce the continent's dependency on aid and instead increase private capital flows, which have declined considerably. Sustainable economic transformation will only be achieved if the leaders and governments in power see the benefits of reforms in terms of removing the structural weaknesses that depress their economies—rather than implementing reforms simply to draw more foreign aid from the Western world. By adopting growth-oriented policies, Africa—as the former World Bank Vice President for Africa, Edward Kim Jaycox, stated during his visit to Kenya—has the capacity to produce the next generation of economic tigers.

Masako Ii

It is a great pleasure for me to be a discussant of the papers by Governor Mwanza from the Bank of Zambia, and Michael Foster from the Overseas Development Administration in London. Since both authors have extensive experience in policymaking, and my background is research oriented, I would like to concentrate my remarks on recent studies on the social impact of adjustment programs. In fact, I am now part of a research group at a Japanese university on the social impact of the structural adjustment, after having worked as a World Bank economist for five years.

My research and field experiences are limited to Latin America and Asian countries, but when I was reading Governor Mwanza's paper on the Zambian economy, I felt as if I were reading an economic report on Bolivia. Both countries are landlocked, and their economic difficulties began when the price of the copper started to decline in the 1970s. So I hope my experiences with Latin American countries can provide some useful suggestions for African policymakers.

To date, a lot of studies have been done on the impact of adjustment programs on social sectors, but some researchers are critical of the findings because the data used for the research have come largely from the IMF's government finance statistics, which covers only central government accounts—not the needed micro-level data. For this reason, I would like to first discuss a 1995 World Bank study that examined the impact of adjustment programs on the health sector, drawing on government spending data at both the national and local levels.[1]

The study looked at 20 countries grouped according to the types of structural adjustment programs: intensive adjustment lending countries and nonintensive adjustment lending countries. Intensive adjustment lending countries were those that received at least two structural adjustment loans or three sectoral adjustment operations, all effective by June 1990 and with the first operation effective by June 1986. These countries are Bolivia, Brazil, Chile, Costa Rica, Kenya, Republic of Korea, Mauritius, Mexico, Philippines, Tunisia, Turkey, and Uruguay. Nonintensive adjustment lending countries were those that had not received adjustment loans by June 1990. These countries are Burkina Faso, Dominican Republic, Egypt, El Salvador, Guatemala, Liberia, Malaysia, and Papua New Guinea.

What is the major finding of the World Bank study? The study found that in both groups, public spending on health as a share of GDP followed a cyclical pattern, declining between 1980 and 1985/86 but rising by 1990. However, the decline was sharper and the recovery was less pronounced and slower in the nonintensive group. A similar pattern was observed in terms of per capita public spending on health.

This finding is contrary to the conventional wisdom that the donor-supported adjustment loan has detrimental effects on health through a reduction in public spending. However, some researchers will also be critical of this study because the sample size was small and the data were outdated. Moreover, because of the lack of data disaggregation, we cannot analyze the effects of adjustment lending on the distribution of spending within the health sector.

What have other studies found? In general, government statistics have shown that social spending did not decrease during the adjustment period, but there were some signs of a misallocation of the social spending. Such expenditures should be targeted at the priority programs that would benefit the poor most—for example, primary education or basic health, and essential drugs and supplies rather than salary supplements within the health program. Thus, further research on this subject is needed since future adjustment programs may need to justify health outlays.

Another result of recent research is that people are willing to pay for the good quality of medical and education services. Indeed, many stud-

---

[1]See Jee-Peng Tang, and others, "Public Spending on Health in the 1980s: the Impact of Adjustment Lending Programs," HCO Dissemination Note No. 61 (Washington: World Bank, 1995).

ies now recommend the introduction of user fees in social sectors—not at the primary level (e.g., primary health care centers), but at the tertiary level (e.g., university hospitals). The revenue raised at the tertiary level could be used for providing primary education and primary health care. Zambia has already started charging user fees and seems to be moving in this direction, but I do not have information on the distribution of spending within the health sector and the education sector. I would like to hear from Governor Mwanza on this point.

In conclusion, I would like to summarize the main findings of the recent research on the impact of adjustment programs as follows:

• The data do not show a major cut in the expenditure share of health and education, but show some expenditure misallocation within a given social sector.

• Trends in public spending alone do not provide a complete picture since most studies have failed to include user fees charged by some institutions and many social services provided by the private sector.

• It is misleading to infer the level and quality of the delivery of social services only from the aggregate spending data.

In closing, I would like to briefly comment on the quality of government statistics. At this stage, the major concerns about adjustment programs in Africa center on the continued low levels of domestic saving ratios and investment—especially private investment—as well as the increased dependence on foreign aid.

But it is possible that official statistics of the international financial institutions, such as the World Bank and the IMF, and African governments underestimate the levels of economic activities, since the data exclude the informal sector. During the described adjustment period, it is likely that economic activities in the informal sector were also stimulated and hence the actual growth and investment may have been greatly underestimated. This measurement error may also be responsible for the pessimism about saving, investment, employment, and growth in African countries.

General Discussion

Getting the Private Sector to Respond

David Cole opened the discussion by noting that Jacob Mwanza's paper about the difficulties that Zambia had encountered over the years made him wonder about the problem of supply response in some African countries—the lack of any palpable improvement two or three years after the restructuring—particularly in the productive, as opposed to the social, sectors.

By contrast, both South Korea in the mid-1960s and Indonesia in the late 1960s had enjoyed fairly rapid supply responses. In South Korea, there had been a rapid response in the industrial sector to the expanding export markets for manufactured goods, with increases in employment and reabsorption of underemployed urban labor. After a slow start, exports grew 40–50 percent a year in 1965–67. In Indonesia, the agricultural sector had been the first to respond, with rice production rising from 9 million tons to 15 million tons over a five-year period, thanks to increased supplies of fertilizer, better transportation, and price stabilization. For both countries, the structural adjustment programs were accepted and had built real political strength for the governments implementing them because of their pervasive effects—in the urban industrial area in South Korea and in the rural agricultural area in Indonesia.

Cole said these cases raised several questions regarding the supply response in Africa. Were the kind of infrastructure and other elements that would support such a rapid supply response much less readily available in Africa?

Luc Oyoubi of Gabon responded that, at least in the case of Gabon, the desired supply response had not been forthcoming either when prices and trade were liberalized in 1989 or when the CFA franc was devalued in 1994, and exports, other than traditional exports, had not risen. Perhaps the problem was that not enough thought had been put into examining the situation before liberalizing the economy. It was as if a nurse had come to heal a wound that had not been properly cleaned, making recovery extremely difficult, if not impossible.

Chérif Bichara of Chad underscored that his country's experience with structural adjustment programs since 1987 demonstrated the importance of communicating with all segments of the population. In 1995, for the first time, the government met with all parties, including the private sector, parliamentarians, and trade unions, in the hope of avoiding any difficulties after the program had been approved. It also took steps to protect the health and education budgets in real terms and create jobs in the urban and suburban areas to reduce unemployment—helped by the initiative of the private sector. In the end, the only people who suffered slightly from structural adjustment were civil servants, whose wages were blocked. All in all, he felt the verdict so far, particularly when it came to health and education, was positive.

Aliou Seck of Senegal seconded the key roles of communication and transparency but questioned the necessity of democracy—defined by him to mean the minority having to abide by the majority. After all, certain Southeast Asian countries had shown that economic progress could be made under military regimes. What was important was that reforms be well explained to the populations, meaning that countries needed to improve their communications policies, and in that regard, African governments would welcome external assistance.

Jack Boorman, who was chairing the session, questioned Seck's interpretation of democracy, suggesting that most people interpret democracy as a system in which the basic rights of minorities are protected. It was not simply a matter of the majority ruling. He also asked how aid agencies and other outsiders could help in fostering the kind of internal dialogue and communication needed to garner support for programs that everybody seemed to agree were necessary.

Seck responded that he was not referring to financial assistance but rather ideas on better ways to communicate. For example, the World Bank had helped with the formation of advisory committees and the like that enabled the government to achieve a consensus on policies and elicit input from the private sector.

Joseph Tsika of Congo argued that it was a bit unfair to compare Africa's situation with that of Southeast Asia, given that enormous sums of financial assistance and investment had been centered on Southeast

Asia, making it possible for that region to accelerate reform, whereas money was no longer flowing to Africa. Donors were telling Africa to become more transparent—which it was doing—and to accelerate reforms, yet the rate at which those reforms could be introduced was being slowed down because of halts in disbursements from donors. Africa was in the midst of a mutation. There had been abuses. But many countries were democratizing their regimes and now needed to handle claims from the military, students, and workers, without any money. What was the solution? Tsika suggested the solution must come from the donors.

Boorman responded by questioning Tsika's proposition that the source of difficulty could be traced to problems with external resource flows. There had been—as recent Development Assistance Committee (DAC) figures showed—a slowdown in aid disbursements around the world. But that was surely not the case in a number of African countries where aid levels had been sustained at fairly high levels.

Said Mondoha of the Comoros said his country's experiences with trying to put together stabilization and structural adjustment programs suggested that the problem lay in failing to take certain political realities into account. Sometimes the government simply could not, or would not, commit to adopting certain measures—such as when the World Bank insisted on the privatization of 1 single company out of 15 while the government felt that it could not commit itself to privatizing that particular company. He also seconded the proposals put forward by Edouard Luboya in the previous day's discussion that the private sector be better taken account of in negotiations. After all, the private sector was a driving force.

Edouard Luboya of Zaïre picked up on the discussion of democracy, observing that, for the private sector, democracy meant a situation in which all parties could freely express themselves—not one where one party was subordinated to another party. Moreover, the government would have to consult with all parties, allowing room for disagreements, and not present the private sector with final decisions, such as on taxes, that would adversely affect those who planned to make needed investments.

As evidence of the private sector's ability to play a key role, he noted that when the government decided to privatize two companies—one handling harbors and ports, and another handling road and river transport—the private sector mobilized so quickly that it was prepared to invest more than what was offered by foreign companies. The same thing happened when it came to privatizing Air Zaïre. A foreign enterprise offered $1 million, whereas local businessmen offered $3 million. Luboya said these examples showed that if the World Bank and IMF would stress the high quality and expertise of the private sector in discussions with the government, the private sector could settle down to solving 50–60 percent of the country's economic problems. There was no time to waste.

Boorman asked Luboya if staff of the World Bank and IMF contacted the National Association of Enterprises or other private sector organizations when they visited Zaïre on missions. Or did the government, after discussions with the institutions, reach out to seek the views of the private sector in any way?

Luboya answered that his presence at the seminar was proof that there was a relationship between his organization and the IMF and the World Bank, at least in recent months. That was why, as in Senegal, there was now a commission—involving the private sector—that dealt with structural reforms.

Ben Ibe of Nigeria raised the question of ownership of adjustment programs, saying that even though such ownership was advocated by the World Bank and the IMF, Nigeria had been trying unsuccessfully since 1994 to get the institutions to accept its three-year medium-term policy adjustment program. It was as if whenever Nigeria wanted to score a goal, the goalpost was moved. And yet without such a program, Nigeria could not hold a dialogue with the Paris Club to reduce its enormous debt. Ibe said he knew Nigeria was not democratic in the way that donors would like it to be, and that it still had a military government in place. But within the system, there was a democracy, and it worked for Nigeria—at least for now, no one was being killed, and the country was stable. Granted, inflation was very high, but the authorities were doing their best to bring it down.

George Anthony Chigora of Zimbabwe noted that the IMF's macroeconomic policy advice had been quite useful, but he also agreed with the sense of shifting goalposts. On many occasions, Zimbabwe felt it had met the expected targets, or at least 90 percent of them, and yet disbursements had not taken place. Some other new issue seemed to suddenly surface. This holdup of a disbursement was not measured or taken into account, yet it negatively affected the economy. In sum, the IMF needed to be more considerate of young economies needing assistance, because the lack of disbursements tended to stifle operations.

Boorman commented at this point that he found both Ibe's and Chigora's comments troubling, as they seemed to imply that there was less than complete understanding between the country and the IMF as to what was expected. The IMF prided itself to a certain extent on transparency, and if they were suggesting that that was not the case, the IMF had to ensure that the situation was corrected.

Peter Warutere of Kenya also expressed frustration with donor conditionality and lack of transparency. In 1993–94, after donors suspended balance of payments aid, the U.S. government withheld $28 million, half of that tied to economic conditions, specifically the maize market, and the other half tied to political conditions. In 1994, Kenya liberalized the maize market, prompting the World Bank and the British to proceed with disbursements tied to that particular economic reform, yet the United States continued to withhold its aid and had yet to disburse.

With parastatal reform, other types of problems arose, such as when there was an agreed program of divestiture or privatization of state investments, but buyers could not be attracted—even after the enterprises had been advertised three or four times. Of course, there were a few that had been sold to the highest bidders, sometimes at less than half the valuation price. However, this had created other problems, with the government being accused of corruption.

Jean-Claude Brou of Côte d'Ivoire observed that the problem was not with the concept of conditionality—everyone agreed that donors should set conditions to ensure that resources made available to support adjustment programs were used in the best possible way, enabling countries to return to external viability. Rather, the real problem was one of pace and approach in implementing the programs. Each donor, whether bilateral or multilateral, gave countries a list of 10–20 conditions to be fulfilled, and some of these, such as structural ones, might be very difficult to implement. In certain cases, objectively, the country had not fulfilled the conditions. But from the start, everyone involved had known that the conditions would require very complex structural measures and adaptations, and perhaps in the end it was not possible, at least not in that time frame. And then without the disbursement, the country did not move forward and obtain external viability, which was the final objective.

Basant Kapur of Singapore closed the session by suggesting that it might be preferable to adopt a more gradual and selective approach to adjustment—first implementing the more narrow economic reforms, such as in trade and finance, and only later implementing the so-called social reforms, such as removing subsidies—to mitigate the impact on disadvantaged groups. There was also a need for reinforcing measures, such as establishing a social safety net to help those who lose their jobs because of privatization. With measures such as retraining programs in place, adjustment programs would stand a much better chance of garnering public support. The seminar participants had discussed the need for dialogue, but dialogue had to be a two-way process, with the legitimate concerns of low-income groups taken into account in the design of programs.

SESSION IV

Future Role of Governments
and Donors

13

Panel Discussion

Mark Baird

What is striking about the discussion at this seminar is the very broad acceptance of the need to go through adjustment. There are clear concerns, however, on the need for both short-term results that can sustain adjustment politically and long-term results that deliver on the sort of reductions in poverty that we are all looking for. And this need raises issues of implementation and supply response.

To be frank, the only way we can resolve this challenge is by being very honest and open about what we do and do not know. And in those areas where we do not have the answers, we really have to work together to find them. Cross-country analysis is a very useful input into that process. But at the end of the day, we are going to have to find solutions for individual countries. One of the things I learned from working on East Asia is that there is no one model even in East Asia. We really do have to find some country-specific answers. That said, there are some general principles we can work from.

All the evidence clearly shows that when you implement sound macroeconomic policies, you do get a supply response. I know the World Bank's 1994 *Adjustment in Africa* study[1] was controversial for many reasons, but on the question of whether there is a supply response to good fiscal policy, good monetary policy, and good exchange rate

---

[1] World Bank, *Adjustment in Africa: Reforms, Results, and the Road Ahead* (Washington: Oxford University Press for the World Bank, 1994).

policy, the supporting evidence in Africa is very strong. We should not lose sight of that important positive message. The report also noted that there has been good progress on macroeconomic policy in Africa. The problem is that the record from country to country is very mixed, and in some countries, there has even been slippage. And as East Asia has shown us, if you do not have that consistency in policy, credibility is very easy to lose. Stability is absolutely critical. Take Indonesia, a country that for 30 years has had one economic team working on economic issues. When a crisis emerges, the team members know exactly what they are going to do in response. There is no hesitancy; there are no mixed signals to the markets. That is the model you need if you want to get a supply response to good macroeconomic policies.

The difficulty, I think, comes when we move on to structural policies. I do not think there is any debate about the direction we want to move on structural reforms—more openness, more liberalization. But there is a debate over timing, pacing, and sequencing. And here, I think, we should be very open about the fact that we do not have one single answer. This is true, for example, for financial sector reform, a topic on which David Cole introduced a healthy note of skepticism into this discussion and where we still have a number of unanswered questions: What do you do when you introduce reforms that have a very sharp impact on interest rates and, potentially, on exchange rates, and can have damaging effects on the banking system, which in turn can feed back into your fiscal problems? As we all know, it is very difficult to find a solution that is consistent with the overall macroeconomic program and will lead to a supply response.

We have heard similar issues raised on both tax reform and on public enterprise reform. On public enterprise reform, for example, the Bank's report *Bureaucrats in Business*[2] has pointed out that if you do not have the preconditions in place in terms of political feasibility, it can be counterproductive to push ahead rapidly with privatization. It does not mean that privatization is not a good thing. It is a good thing. But the question is: Do you have the conditions in place? John Nellis told us about alternatives, such as management contracts and leases. Do we really have the full agenda of options laid out? This was brought home to me when I worked on a couple of adjustment programs—in Indonesia, where the current account was opened up early on in the reform program, and my orthodoxy told me you should open up the current account later; and subsequently in my home country, New Zealand, where again in a reform program the current account was

---

[2]World Bank, *Bureaucrats in Business: The Economics and Politics of Government Ownership* (Washington: Oxford University Press for the World Bank, 1995).

opened up early on. Clearly we should not be too dogmatic about what is the precise answer. Let us try to find what will work in a particular country situation. The key here is surely consistency. If you are going to take a given approach to interest rates, exchange rates, and financial sector reform, make sure the reforms are internally consistent, because if they are not, they will not be credible.

That brings me to the final and, I think, the most difficult question: Should the government actually go further than structural reforms to promote the private sector? I think one thing we have learned is that it is not a simple matter of putting the public sector role on one side of the ledger and the private sector on the other. It is really the interface between the two that gives us a good result. We are learning a lot about the role of the public sector in providing the regulatory legal framework for the private sector. But we also know that the bureaucratic requirements of implementing these types of policies are very demanding. Moreover, in Africa, where the need for government intervention is probably very strong, the ability to deliver it is very weak. The interesting question then becomes not so much *what* should the government do, but *how* can we improve the government's capacity to do what it has to. And there I honestly believe that although we have come some way in understanding, we are not yet applying that understanding consistently across countries.

We have heard a number of radical solutions to improving government capacity—"abolishing" the customs administration in Indonesia is one. However, there are other less radical, but I think equally important, changes that can be made—paying customs officials high salaries to avoid corruption, or breaking down the face-to-face relationship between the customs officers and the client through the use of computer technology. These kind of changes can make a real difference.

We have also heard about changes in budget management. This is a critical area. In the past, I think we have spent too much time looking at ways of improving accounting systems without paying sufficient attention to the incentives that underlie budget management. And there are other ideas about how one can depoliticize the budget process through fiscal responsibility legislation and budget laws, ideas we need to be bringing much more directly into the debate.

At the end of the day, however, we have to find answers that will meet the needs of the African clients. Within the World Bank, I can assure you that we are now giving a lot more research attention to these problems. As Michael Bruno, the Chief Economist, has made clear, this is a challenge we accept. But I think to work it through, we are going to have to come and talk to all of you to help us get the agenda right, collect the appropriate evidence, and reach the right conclusions.

Aid Effectiveness

Let me now turn to the issue of aid effectiveness in Africa, where we have very high net disbursements of aid with a perception of very limited results. Net overseas development assistance to Africa, actual disbursements less actual repayments, is now about 12 percent of GDP in these countries. It is higher than it was in the past, and it is substantially higher than it is in other regions. Yet when we look at all the studies trying to assess the impact of aid, we find that they often come out with very weak or mixed results, and that in turn affects our ability to mobilize aid. It is also a serious concern for African countries—if they are borrowing money, even on concessional terms, and not generating results, it is contributing to the type of debt problem they face. This is the crux of the aid effectiveness issue and one that we have to address up front. When we come to specific countries and specific projects, the results are often more promising. What we need to do is work from those to try and better understand what we can do to improve the overall impact of aid. Let me make four points.

First, we cannot get away from the fact that policy does matter for the effectiveness of aid. We have a number of studies that now show this—the last report of the Operations Evaluation Department of the World Bank,[3] for example, clearly links the returns on World Bank projects with the policy environment in which they take place. We can try to isolate projects from bad policy, but even in doing that we create problems—drawing resources and limited staff away from other needs. We also have to worry about what we are really financing at the margin—the fungibility issue. That is why you are seeing a lot more focus now on overall expenditure programs as a means of getting a much more complete view of what is happening in the budgets and in the aid programs. This leads, of course, to the conclusion that we will be more selective in the countries that we support. I know that is a controversial suggestion. Good performers like it; not-so-good performers are less keen on it. But in a world of limited resources it is a reality we have to face.

Second, if we accept the proposition that policy matters, I would argue that adjustment lending has been an important instrument to achieve better policy. The problem is that adjustment lending can become very addictive in itself, and if we provide adjustment lending in countries where policy reform is not strong, then we get very limited results and give the instrument itself a bad name.

We have to improve the instrument. Ravi Kanbur has been pushing us very hard within the Bank to change our approach to adjustment

---

[3]World Bank, *Annual Review of Evaluation Results, 1994* (Washington: World Bank, Operations Evaluations Department, November 10, 1995).

lending, and he has had some success. We now have much greater recognition of the value of single tranche operations, based on up-front policy actions—as opposed to multiple tranche operations, where money is disbursed as conditions are met. We have simplified disbursement procedures. We are recognizing the fiscal rationale as well as the balance of payments rationale for adjustment lending. We hope these changes give you an instrument that is more responsive to your needs, and we would welcome feedback in terms of how it works.

Third, it is very clear that we have to spend a lot more time up front developing the local capacity and consensus for reform. As you know, [World Bank President] Mr. Wolfensohn has given a high priority to expanding the role of the Economic Development Institute. EDI is working very actively building capacity and consensus; holding seminars with parliamentarians and trade unions; and discussing sensitive issues like governance, which we cannot tackle through many of our normal instruments. I would urge you to take advantage of it as a potentially important tool for building local capacity.

Finally, let me turn to the issue of coordination. I think that within the World Bank Group we need a much more coherent approach to the way we look at countries. For example, we have something like 35 groups working on private sector development—which is simply unacceptable, and we will be coming up with a much more coherent approach. Country Assistance Strategies are being used as one instrument for getting there, as they offer a very useful instrument for coming to a consistent view of what the Bank Group is going to do in a country. More investment in these strategies would give us much more flexibility in how we use different instruments—both lending and nonlending—to support country programs. I also hear the message on Policy Framework Papers. If we do have issues in terms of the timing and sequencing of structural reforms, if there are concerns on the social impact of adjustment programs, clearly we have to work together both with the country and the IMF early on in the process to resolve them, and the Policy Framework Paper provides us with one instrument that we should probably use more actively to that end.

Richard Carey

I would like to start by going back to Kwesi Botchwey's text of yesterday morning, which gave us a brilliant start to this seminar. Specifically, I would like to go back to the rather basic point he made that, to the extent that structural reform programs provide the overall policy framework for domestic policy reform and external resource transfers, these programs must be strengthened in their design, negotiation, and implementation so as to facilitate the realization of the fundamental goals of economic development.

The design, negotiation, and implementation of structural reform programs so as to facilitate the realization of the fundamental goals of economic development—that is an agenda that we have been working on in the Development Assistance Committee (DAC) for over a decade. I have been listening to the proceedings of this seminar very carefully because they have been an important reflection of the state of play on this agenda, helping us to see where we are now and how we can move forward on some key fronts.

The DAC has produced a number of guidelines that are particularly relevant in this context. They relate to aid coordination, program assistance principles, participatory development and good governance, and private sector development. The latest in this series of conceptual and policy guidance pieces was produced just a week ago at the annual DAC high-level meeting in Paris, which brought together aid ministers and heads of aid agencies. It is a major policy statement called "Shaping the 21st Century: The Contribution of Development Cooperation."

What this statement does is to set out a vision in the form of human development objectives for the year 2015 for the reduction of poverty, educational attainment, gender equality, population stabilization, environmental sustainability, and so on. The targets specified are all drawn from the outcomes of UN conferences held over the last few years. They are not very new or controversial in the development debate. But they serve an important inspirational purpose. What they do is to say that this is the kind of world we would like to see when we look at the social indicators in 2015 and, taxpayers of the OECD countries, this is the outcome your money contributes to when you fund aid programs.

Alongside this vision of development progress into the next century, the other major element of the DAC policy statement is a sketch of a concept of development partnerships. This term "development partnerships" was mentioned yesterday by Michael Foster. The question is: What does it mean? It is, of course, a very nice phrase, and that is one reason why it is used. But there is some important substance behind it, and it is substance that we have been discussing in one way or another over the last day or so.

Development Partnerships

The term development partnerships derives from four major changes in perspective.

First, we have all now moved from looking at conditionality as a cost of access to external resources to thinking in terms of policy reform as the path to sustainable development. This meeting and other meetings of this kind reflect a major transition in thinking among developing countries themselves, among Africans themselves. This was the point made by Mark Baird. We are not talking any more about whether to engage in policy reform, but how to do it. And Africans themselves are now fully engaged in the issues of design, negotiation, and implementation. As we have learned today, this is not a matter just for a narrow group of politicians or officials, but something that is reaching out now quite deeply into African societies and has to reach out into African societies.

The *second* change is that *we have shifted from short-term adjustment perspectives to long-term perspectives and a concern with sustainability*— economic, social, environmental, cultural, and political. And we have all come to see the key importance of institutional and capacity development in the reform process.

The perception that institutions and capacity are fundamental for sustainable policy reform and adjustment has been having a major impact on donor thinking, both in bilateral agencies and in the multilateral agencies, including the World Bank. The shift, for example, from an approvals culture to a results culture in the Bank and other aid agencies is based on this perception. Aid agencies and their staffs will need to have different incentives and performance objectives, with less emphasis on negotiating new commitments and more on fostering implementation capacity and effectively functioning institutional arrangements.

Our longer-term perspective has also meant a widening of the agenda of development strategies and of development cooperation. We are dealing with a much wider range of substantive issues now. So, again, the institutional and capacity development objective means longer-term partnerships and different ways of working together with wider participation from within developing countries.

Third, the results culture itself brings new perspectives in the aid community and in the international financial institutions regarding coordination, both within the donor community and with the recipient country. If you think in terms of results, it is the total effort of all actors that counts, not just your effort. So you have to be much more concerned with coordination issues, with what it is all adding up to. The results culture is also leading toward integrated sector approaches because a results culture has to go beyond the project, looking at results over five, ten years. What counts here is building capacity in broad sectors and getting resource allocation by both donors and recipients to match with priorities.

Thus, the partnership approach also derives, as a *fourth* change, from *a shift in accountability philosophies,* particularly accountability philosophies on balance of payments and budget support. Accountability in balance of payments support was until very recently done by trying to attach money to particular imports and so forth, which as good economists we all know is totally fictitious. We are now seeing accountability for these broad kinds of financial support in terms of government priorities. What is being done with these resources in terms of resource allocation, particularly through the public budget?

So I think these are four key reasons why we are now in a different era in terms of relationships between the donor community and the recipient countries.

New DAC Initiatives

Next, I would like to mention some practical initiatives that the DAC is taking to improve overseas development assistance, but first a word about the current environment in which we must operate.

The interface between donors and recipient countries is a complicated one. The reform process itself is complicated. The aid process is complicated because there are many actors. Each actor has a different set of operational modalities, different conditions, coming often from different angles. We have also moved way beyond the two-gap model, which provided the conceptual framework for consultative group meetings, for example. The agendas of consultative group meetings have widened. They include governance, financial sector reform, private sector reform, human development—all the things we have been discussing today.

We also have donors pressing developing countries to improve the rationality and efficiency of public management. At the same time, we are increasingly aware that the donor community can itself be a source of irrationality and inefficiency in public management in developing countries. How could it be otherwise when we have so many actors providing resources in so many different ways with so many different requirements along the way? We have the problem of budget fragmentation. We have the problem of multiplication of procedures and conditionality, the problem that ministers end up by being "Ministers of Donor Projects," as Michael Foster said yesterday.

We are taking a number of initiatives in the DAC to see if we can work on these issues. First of all, we are going to undertake a *developing-country-based aid review*. We will try to assess how the aid system as a whole is functioning in one country, not in narrow "does aid produce growth" terms, but rather more operational terms. Thus, we will be looking at the impact of the aid system on the functioning of the state, on the functioning of the private sector, and on the functioning of civil society. And we will be doing this through an in-country process. Government officials, the World Bank, UNDP, and donor field offices will first of all put together an overall assessment. We will then have a panel of senior donor officials that will look at the results and discuss them with ministers of the country concerned. We are hoping to do a first pilot review in Mali, and I was talking yesterday with Soumaïla Cissé about doing that.

The second initiative is in the area of *governance*. The DAC has compiled guidelines on participatory development and good governance, which are programmatic in character; that is to say, they try to look at these issues in practical ways. They identify institution-building implications of good governance and the ways in which the donor community can help to build those institutions. There is also an inherent philosophy about the kinds of dialogue that the donor and recipient countries could have. What we have done most recently—and agreed at our high-level meeting last week—is to write a policy note on improving country-level coordination and consultation on good governance to provide guidance at the field level.

What is foreseen here is to help foster an in-country process of discussing governance issues and then to bring the results of that discussion to the consultative group and roundtable meetings. We are all aware that governance issues are now very pervasive in consultative group meetings, but they are handled in a rather unsystematic way. What we would like is to see better prepared consultative group meeting agendas, so that we have a more focused and contained discussion and, we would hope, a more productive one. We believe this would help the efficiency of the consultative group process overall because, as I have said, there are many agenda items that are starting to crowd into these consultative group meetings now.

The third area in which we are undertaking an initiative is improving the effectiveness of *technical cooperation*. Much technical cooperation in the past has not managed to build sustainable capacity. We have been asking why. And we have been looking at best practices, at ways of cooperating that would produce lasting results.

We are also looking at the impact of donor practices in technical cooperation on local labor markets in developing countries. If donors come in and hire away talent that should be working in local institutions—rather than hijacked by the donor community—then we are getting a perverse impact from the way in which we are conducting the aid process. This is a very, very difficult topic, but it is one that we are trying to look at.

Finally, we also would see the technical cooperation/institution-building issues being brought into consultative group meetings in a more systematic way than they have been in the past. There have been too many consultative group meetings on public investment programs and policy reforms with institution-building implications that have never been made explicit, never been adequately programmed.

So, Mr. Chairman, those are just some of the practical initiatives that I wanted to tell this meeting about. I have profited greatly from the discussion here and will be carrying back many of the messages that I have heard into the DAC processes.

Ravi Kanbur

The government of Japan has started a remarkable dialogue here through this series of conferences between Asia and Africa, and over the last two or three conferences, I have sensed a maturing and a deepening of the dialogue that is taking place. I think we are realizing that there is not *the* East Asian miracle; there are many East Asian miracles, each with their own peculiarities. And, of course, there is not a single Africa; there are many Africas. As we point out in our latest report, *A Continent in Transition,*[1] which was presented in Tokyo in April, the differentiation is in some sense what characterizes Africa now. Country specificity should be the basis of our discussion and dialogue.

Another sign of the dialogue maturing and deepening is that there are more questions than answers around the table. I do not think there is anything wrong with that. Some searching questions are being asked. And listening to what was being discussed, I picked out three issues that I think merit more discussion and more dialogue: *culture, timing,* and *conditionality.*

The Issue of Culture

I think all of us would accept that culture is important. The question is how exactly is it important. And there are many paradoxes around. First, Tetsuji Tanaka mentioned Confucian values, and many commentators today attribute the success of some East Asian countries to Confucian values. But those of you who remember texts from 40–50 years ago, might recall that those texts, in fact, were saying that the reason for East Asia's *slow* progress was Confucian values. So what is going on in this context?

---

[1]Kevin Cleaver, Ravi Kanbur, and Mustapha Rouis, *A Continent in Transition: Sub-Saharan Africa in the Mid-1990s* (Washington: World Bank, Africa Region, 1995).

Second, we heard from Dahlan Sutalaksana and David Cole about the remarkable advances in Indonesia in terms of rice production among the peasants, a jump from 9 million tons in a period of five years. Yet 40–50 years ago, the famous Dutch anthropologist Boeke coined the term "the dual economy" to describe what he saw as the disconnect between the Indonesian peasantry—whom he described as being seen in shadows and silhouettes in the background—and what he thought of as being a modern economy.

Third, for those of you who remember Gunnar Myrdal's famous book, *Asian Drama,*[2] where the negative weight of culture on Asian development was prominent, just look at Bangalore in India, where the Silicon Valley of India is developing.

So how exactly cultures affect development, I think, is something we do not understand, and as a group we should continue to discuss.

The Issue of Timing

On timing, certainly Yasuo Yokoyama's point about the desirability of countries taking some 50 years to establish sound economic fundamentals before proceeding with privatization evoked a response from our African colleagues, and there is a real issue here in the sense that, indeed, many elements of the East Asian success took a long time. And 50 years ago, we might have had 50 years; but I think the African reality is that we do not now have 50 years. Moreover, what our African colleagues are telling us is that they are looking for quick results over a 5- to 7-year horizon, not a 15- to 20- to 25-year horizon.

That raises some paradoxes and some dilemmas. I agree very much with David Cole in terms of some of his skepticism about quick movement on the financial reform front. But while agreeing with that, David, I would still then pose the question back to you: How do we respond to the demand for quick growth? Quick financial reform may not be the right way to go, but then what is the right way to go? Again, I think there are more questions here than answers.

The Issue of Conditionality

On conditionality, we have come a long way in terms of our discussion on this issue, and the World Bank has learned very painfully that without government consensus and government ownership nothing will happen. These conditionalities are meant to be part of legal con-

---

[2]Gunnar Myrdal, *Asian Drama: An Inquiry into the Poverty of Nations* (New York: Twentieth Century Fund, 1968).

tracts, meant to be imposed by the Bretton Woods institutions. But if you look at compliance rates on these conditionalities, they are running at about 40–50 percent, and yet not very many tranches have been left unreleased.

So what is going on? There are paradoxes here in terms of conditionality, ownership, and policy reform—paradoxes galore in the East Asian context. One of the major elements of success that Western commentators cite is land reform, and yet, as we know, in many cases this land reform was imposed by an occupying military power. So I am not sure that we fully understand all the interactions.

Kwesi Botchwey mentioned the peculiar difficulties that the adjustment lending instrument has as we move into the deeper reform agenda, as we move into areas of reform that are very tricky, politically and technically. To link those conditions to a macroeconomic program where you have to deliver—where the resources should be delivered in a sustained and predictable manner is a major problem. It is a technical design problem that we are trying to address, but it is also a basic issue: suppose there is disagreement between the government and the donors, what happens? Ben Ibe from Nigeria mentioned that Nigeria has its own homegrown program. Presumably, there is ownership. But it is not acceptable to the donor community. What do you do then in that context?

These problems will not go away, but I think we can solve some of them through technical solutions of the type that Mark Baird mentioned, where you try to disconnect the resource flow from the specific satisfaction of specific conditionalities in tricky areas, such as civil service reform, privatization, and so on.

But then if you move away from that, what do you replace it with? How can donors get a handle on whether or not things are moving in the country? What is the framework in which you discuss this? I would fully support Botchwey's proposal that we move away from the very specific link between specific conditions and specific disbursements—instead adopting a broader framework where there is a three- to five-year agreement on a broad program, including a broad assessment of whether or not that program is successful. But I am afraid that will, in fact, raise even more questions, such as what that broad assessment should be. Suppose there is a disagreement between the broad assessment of the government and the broad assessment of the donors? Then what happens in that context? So I think we are making some progress but, as always, there are more questions than answers.

Just let me conclude by saying that the dialogue is maturing and deepening, and what is needed now is much more detailed country-specific discussions both among policymakers from Asia and Africa, and among scholars from Asia and Africa.

Hiroyuki Hino

In preparation for this seminar, I asked desk economists in the IMF to list three or four key concerns of bilateral donors in the African countries where an IMF-supported program is in place or where there are reasonable prospects for such a program in the near future. Governance was seen as a key concern of bilateral donors for as many as two-thirds of the countries surveyed. In certain instances where concerns on governance became acute, bilateral donors sharply cut back their assistance, particularly their balance of payments support. One example is the case of Kenya, which Peter Warutere mentioned yesterday. This highlights the importance of governance in donor-recipient relations today.

Governance encompasses an array of issues, including not only those that directly involve financial implications—such as corruption, lack of transparency in budgetary procedures, and an ineffective judicial system in relation to commercial and financial activities—but also those that are more political in nature, such as democratization, the political process, the administration of justice as related to human rights, and freedom of the press.

Economic and Noneconomic Governance

There is now a growing consensus that economic governance is an important factor affecting investment, savings, and economic growth in many African countries. A prospective investor will be reluctant to invest in a country where his competitors may be granted special favors, such as exemption from tax payments and preferential access to government contracts. Similarly, if contractual obligations cannot be enforced or if property rights are not very secure in a country because of an inadequate judicial system, investors might prefer to invest or save in more secure locations. There are indications that these factors—which lead to an absence of adequate economic security—have adversely affected private investment and savings in a number of African countries. During the last three years, net private capital inflows to the sub-Saharan African countries (excluding Angola, Nigeria, and South Africa) amounted to only $0.5–1.0 billion annually. The absence of adequate economic security explains in part these low private capital inflows.

Some dismiss corruption as an important macroeconomic issue, stating that the problem is universal and that a number of countries have grown rapidly despite widespread corruption. This argument overlooks the concern that the efficiency of resource allocation is undermined by corruption. In fact, Dahlan Sutalaksana referred to a similar problem in Indonesia as a nonmarket allocation of rent, which he said is a source of high economic cost and weakens the competitive effect of market mechanisms.

Therefore, when economic governance leads to problems that entail macroeconomic implications, it is important to address this issue as a key element of the economic reform agenda. The remedy could involve a number of measures, such as (1) closing avenues for rent seeking; (2) stablishing a system that would assure full transparency in public finance, including budgetary processes; (3) strictly enforcing a civil service code of conduct, which includes, where appropriate, dismissal and prosecution of officials involved in financial malpractice; and (4) establishing a civil service that is lean, efficient, and properly remunerated.

The relationship between noneconomic governance issues and economic performance is more complex. In 1993, Singapore's Senior Minister, Lee Kuan Yew, told the Africa Leadership Forum that good government is necessary for economic development, but that good government is not necessarily good governance as defined by Western donors. Some participants in our seminar noted yesterday that Korea and Taiwan, for example, developed initially under a political system that might not be viewed by donor countries as representing good governance. Some African observers also wonder whether democracy of the Westminster type is a necessary ingredient for economic development in all the African countries. What is the meaning of casting a vote when you have nothing to lose or protect? Can a nation with a mature political system be created instantly if its national boundaries were artificially drawn only recently? It has been suggested by some observers that in Africa, it may not be appropriate to adopt a multiparty political system at an early stage of a country's development because such a system could sharpen tribal conflict. If this consideration is valid, then economic reforms should precede political reforms, rather than being pursued simultaneously.

There is of course an opposing view, namely, that good political governance is essential for good economic performance. Jacob Mwanza mentioned yesterday that Zambia was able to introduce tough adjustment measures only because its president was recently elected by popular vote and had a mandate for such reform. The transition in Malawi also appears to have helped to reinvigorate the adjustment process. It could be argued in these cases that public participation in policy decision making, which is inherent in the democratic process, has enhanced the political support for economic reform. In some other countries, it is believed that political reconciliation among rival parties would help enhance political stability and, hence, investor confidence. Indeed, the prevalent view in the bilateral donor community, according to a recent OECD document, is that "it has become increasingly apparent that there is a vital connection between open, democratic and accountable systems of governance and respect for human rights and the ability to achieve sustained economic and social development."[1] A number of bilateral donors who are facing increasingly severe budgetary constraints are directly linking their assistance to the political aspects of good governance.

Sub-Saharan Africa still depends heavily on donor assistance. In several countries, net flows of official resources are estimated at the equivalent of more than 20 percent of GDP in 1995. This means that African countries need to develop a constructive approach to deal with a broad range of governance issues that bilateral donors consider important. Richard Carey discussed the approaches that the bilateral donors may be adopting in this regard.

As for the IMF, its discussions with member countries will focus on economic governance, insofar as governance affects macroeconomic performance. It will certainly need to be aware of the sensitivities involved, and to ensure that discussions are based on facts, not rumors. Moreover, it is necessary to ensure that due process—administrative or judicial—is not undermined as a result of an interaction between the international institutions and their member countries.

The IMF does not have a mandate to address governance issues that do not involve macroeconomic implications. However, if bilateral assistance is disrupted because of donor concerns and financial resources become insufficient to adequately fund a structural adjustment program, a country's financial arrangement with the IMF would be interrupted. As it is crucial to avoid such interruptions in the structural reform efforts and in the associated donor inflows of financing, I would support what many of the seminar participants have emphasized in the discussion today: African governments should engage in a dialogue with bilateral donors so as to address their concerns in a manner that is mutually acceptable.

---

[1]OECD, *Participatory Development and Good Governance*, Development Cooperation Guidelines Series, Development Assistance Committee (Paris: OECD, 1995).

14

Tour de Table

I N THE FINAL tour de table, several key themes emerged.

Culture

On the question of culture, *Jacob Mwanza* of Zambia observed that the seminar had opened a window of opportunity for his country and the African continent to explore economic models of development that stood as alternatives to the traditional Western ones. Development across cultures was possible, with the success stories sharing one key element: the consistent pursuit and implementation of sound macroeconomic policies.

The openness to drawing on the best from each culture was shared by *Jean-Claude Brou* of Côte d'Ivoire, who emphasized that every culture had something to offer in terms of facilitating economic development. In the design of long-term programs in African economies, one needed to draw on the best elements of African cultures.

Toshio Fujinuma of Japan cautioned, however, that taking culture into account did not mean just picking the best model for rapid economic growth but, rather, instigating changes in social values or behavior patterns—in other words, totally changing the whole social system, not just the economic system. It was very tempting and easy for donors to try to insist on certain social or behavioral changes, but more likely the answer laid in recipient countries generating these changes on their own.

Hitoshi Shimura of Japan also underscored that before Japan could agree to particular aid packages, it would first have to bring its taxpayers on board. To do that, he conceded, Japan would need to better understand African countries, not just in economic terms but also in political and cultural terms.

East Asian Miracle

Drawing lessons from the East Asian miracle, *Basant Kapur* of Singapore emphasized the importance of an outward-oriented trade and investment strategy to boost economic efficiency and competitiveness. Such a strategy involved many elements, such as getting prices right, pursuing wide-ranging economic and social infrastructure improvements, attracting direct foreign investment (which brought not only capital but also technology and access to foreign markets), and insisting on good governance.

Tetsuji Tanaka of Japan noted, however, that the exact recipe would vary from country to country, reflecting diverse starting points and differences among countries, such as in culture. As a result, each country would have to bear a different cost and adopt its own speed in the move to a market economy. Even so, he was confident that Africa as a whole would emerge as a major economic power in the 21st century.

Governance

The need for good governance was stressed by *Joseph Kinyua* of Kenya, who considered it a critical element of deepening structural reform in Africa—which in turn was essential for reducing poverty on a long-lasting basis. Picking up on Hiroyuki Hino's distinction between economic and noneconomic governance in the prior panel discussion, he remarked that a lack of good economic governance gave rise to wasted resources and investment distortions, making it harder for policymakers to raise living standards. But it was difficult to achieve good economic governance without also securing good noneconomic governance, which formed the basis for political stability.

Brou suggested that many African countries were making progress on the economic governance front—making budgetary procedures more transparent, improving economic security, and fighting corruption. Indeed, these were essential components of most African countries' economic programs aimed at boosting economic efficiency. Progress made on the noneconomic governance front, such as the democratic process, should help improve the implementation of economic reform programs.

Peter Warutere of Kenya called upon African governments to act on some basic issues being cited in negotiations with donors, such as utilization of revenue, enforcement of the civil service code, and prosecution of public servants who were involved in corruption. However, that should be done because governments felt accountable to use the judicial systems to prosecute such issues, and not just because donors insisted on those actions before providing aid.

Luc Oyoubi of Gabon wondered whether everyone in the seminar meant the same thing when they talked about democracy, as some seemed to feel that there were only good elements. Certainly, freedom of enterprise was favorable, but output lost to strikes was not.

Conditionality

From the donor point of view, *Michael Foster* of the United Kingdon commented that a major problem he observed with conditionality was that it prevented credibility. It was private investors, not donors, who needed to be convinced and, with that in mind, calling economic programs "IMF and World Bank programs" was quite unhelpful. Recipient governments should take ownership of their programs and convince private investors that they would remain committed.

The importance of ownership and commitment was also mentioned by *Gebreselassie Yosief* of Eritrea, who said that the recent experiences of his newborn nation illustrated that those elements mattered far more than conditionality. Although Eritrea had yet to draw on much external support, it had moved quickly with homegrown policies to liberalize trade and investment, create a lean, efficient government, and privatize state enterprises—a sharp contrast to other countries with Policy Framework Papers on the books but never actually implemented.

David Cole of the United States counseled that the relationship between the providers of external financing and technical assistance and the recipients had the best chance of succeeding when it was seen as an alliance rather than an adversarial relationship. So long as it was structured on adversarial grounds, there were going to be problems. As evidence he cited the cases of Korea in the mid-1960s and Indonesia in the late 1960s, both of which enjoyed turning points when there was a close alliance between donors and recipients.

Timing

What would the timing be for Africa? *Brou*—reacting to Yasuo Yokoyama's statement that countries should spend decades establishing sound economic fundamentals before embarking on privatizations, as Japan had done—stressed that Africa could not afford the luxury to wait that long to replicate the East Asian miracle. It could not allow itself that luxury. Already, there were positive stirrings in several countries in East, West, and South Africa. Africa was a mutating continent, a continent in transition, now going through the difficulties that East Asia and others had experienced on their own road to development.

Cole cautioned, however, that in the 1950s and 1960s, the symbol of development and modernization had been the steel mill, leading many countries to feel that if they built a steel mill they would be industrialized and well on the road to development. He worried that in the 1990s, Africans had come to view the establishment of securities markets as a symbol of modernization of the financial system—a leap that could be taken—when in reality, there were many intermediate steps, and countries had to weigh comparative advantage, capacity, and real economic needs before deciding on a financial sector strategy.

This note of caution was echoed by *Tadahiko Nakagawa* of Japan, who mentioned that even if an issue is burning, we must think first. Nonetheless, he underscored the international community's responsibility to help Africa in its time of need, looking for optimism in the fact that many Africans at the seminar had cited growing signs of private sector development.

15

Concluding Remarks

Jack Boorman

THE AGENDA for this seminar reflected a presumption that there is
now an acceptance of the proposition that a continued stable
macroeconomic environment—as illustrated by the comments on Indonesia—is a prerequisite for rapid economic growth. I think that presumption has been fully endorsed.

This is, of course, one of the key lessons of the Asian miracle. Indeed,
East Asia has many lessons to offer, demonstrating the need for, and the
rewards from, high levels of savings and investment, budget discipline,
and relatively low inflation rates—all essential ingredients in establishing
an environment conducive to a dynamic private sector and to growth.

But does this mean Africa can simply copy what worked best in East
Asia and hope for a similar takeoff in the years to come? This is one of
the issues underlying the debate this year, as well as in the previous
seminars.

What seems to come out of this discussion is that the economic environment has changed dramatically since the East Asian countries established the basis for their spectacular growth. In a world of economic
globalization and integrated financial markets—not to mention the sea
change in the prospects for private capital flows—one must ask whether
the relative costs and benefits for Africa of opening up its markets only
slowly are the same as those faced in Asia when countries in that region
took their decisions regarding liberalization. We all know the figures.
Last year, for example, there were $60 billion in official assistance and
about $200 billion in private flows—three times the amount of official
assistance. This reality has, I believe, changed the rules of the game and,

importantly, the opportunities that are available to developing countries. But I agree with David Cole that this does not necessarily mean a portfolio investment market is needed. It does mean, however, an openness to various kinds of flows, particularly private direct investment flows.

The message that came through this discussion seemed to be that the cost of acting slowly—and forgoing the benefits that faster access to outside capital and technology can provide—is too dear. The warnings of David Cole of misstepping in the liberalization process are well taken, but I believe that most here want to see as rapid progress as possible, consistent with the maintenance of sound and stable financial systems.

We are having this debate at a time when, after years of trying to stabilize economies that have been battered by terms-of-trade shocks, by civil strife, and by economic mismanagement, many African countries are finally turning in positive growth rates. Hopefully, we are seeing the end of the long decline in per capita income levels in so many African countries.

Macroeconomic stabilization has played an important role in this reversal. That is clearly something we have learned how to do, and its results are, as Mark Baird has said, becoming increasingly evident. But at the same time, by now we had hoped for better results. Growth simply has to be higher. Real progress in the closing of the ever-widening gap between Africa and much of the rest of the world will require much higher growth rates. The supply side of economies is responding, but it needs to respond even faster!

How do we do that? Looking across the African continent, countries have, by and large, been reasonably successful in implementing what may be described as "early stage" structural reforms. They have reformed the exchange rate systems, opened the trade and payment systems, removed price controls, and liberalized production and marketing systems, especially in the agricultural sector.

These reforms are all essential prerequisites. But the record on the more difficult reforms—involving revenue mobilization, public enterprises, privatization, and the financial sector—has been much more uneven. Moreover, as banking systems have run into problems—and we know that that is the case in all too many countries, not just Africa—some observers have questioned whether the initial liberalization might have been too rapid. That is why we cast the agenda for this seminar around the themes of accelerating structural reform in these various areas.

My sense from the response of our African friends is that we struck a nerve here—that it is precisely these issues with which you are wrestling at home! There seems to be a general acceptance of the need to press firmly on with market-based monetary and exchange management and the promotion of sound financial systems, but with the coherence and sustained commitment and with the prerequisites in place that those kinds of reforms require. There is also a need for the attendant legal and institutional changes. Only through such measures can we ensure efficiency in resource allocation, attract foreign investment, and foster the much-needed domestic savings and investment that ultimately hold the key to the faster growth everyone is seeking.

But how should these reforms be sequenced? And what is the optimal pace of reform, both within sectors and across sectors? Some of you clearly favored a more gradual approach, while others opted for moving as quickly as possible and on as many fronts as possible—especially if there was the political will to do so. Indeed, a quick move to more market-oriented policies can sometimes depersonalize and depoliticize the reform process in a very helpful way. But on this issue, as on others, I think semantics tend to disguise how much common ground there is within the group.

One unmistakable message to be taken from this discussion is that the politics of structural reform are tough and that more effort must go into communicating the cost and benefits of policy options. For structural adjustment programs generally, as several speakers noted, more effort needs to go into explaining the short-term costs as well as the medium- and long-term gains that are hoped for from such programs. Several of our African colleagues have indicated that they now have a clearer vision of the steps that must be taken—much as the East Asian policymakers had been convinced of the steps they needed to take at various critical turns in their economic development.

But it is also clear that, more than ever before, there is a strong need for policymakers to engage in a dialogue with their own civil societies—especially the private sector, which has a vital role to play in fostering economic growth—to assure that these groups are brought along with the reform process and not surprised by measures. For example, as a number of speakers pointed out, privatization is not an easy issue to sell to labor unions and other vested interests in the parastatal sector. In these cases, the cost of inefficiencies and inaction must be clearly spelled out. We all heard the plea that the donor community and the multilateral institutions could help by being more sensitive to the fact that this is a difficult social and political issue, not just a technical one.

More generally, as the dialogue with civil society is stepped up, the pressures for democratization and good governance will grow. My sense from the discussions here is that there is widespread acceptance of the view that good governance—defined to include greater transparency and accountability in the life of governments—is desirable and, inevitably, a legitimate concern of donors. At the same time, there is a need to find new ways to craft programs and sector projects to assure donors that their monies are being put to good use, while—and here is the trick—at the same time permitting governments to retain "ownership" of their reforms, ownership being emphasized by many around the table as absolutely critical to successful reform efforts.

However, there is also the view that governance and democracy are not the same thing and that there needs to be more exploration, country by country, and perhaps with more subtlety, in the search for democratic processes appropriate to the conditions of Africa. There is also a need to take seriously the concern expressed here that the treatment of countries on such sensitive issues as human rights be consistent.

Which leads me to my final thought. With a consensus now on the stabilization and structural measures that need to be taken to ensure sustainable growth and prosperity, what should we be debating? I believe Mark Baird and Ravi Kanbur hit the nail on the head, and I would subscribe to putting more energy into understanding individual country circumstances—debating with policymakers, NGOs, the private sector, and all interested parties on how best to proceed, what the appropriate pace of reform can be, and what institutional environment needs to be in place to proceed from one reform to the next. Indeed, country specificity needs more and more to be the focus of our dialogue.

List of Participants

Chairmen

Jack Boorman
Director
Policy Development and Review
Department
International Monetary Fund

Hideichiro Hamanaka
Deputy Director General
International Finance Bureau
Ministry of Finance
Japan

Speakers

Mark Baird
Director
Development Policy
World Bank

Kwesi Botchwey
Visiting Scholar and Development
  Advisor at the Harvard Institute for
  International Development and
  formerly Minister of Finance for Ghana
Ghana

Jean-Claude Brou
Director of Prime Minister's Cabinet
  and Chairman of the Privatization
  Committee
Côte d'Ivoire

Richard Carey
Deputy Director
Development Assistance Committee
Organization for Economic Cooperation
  and Development

Soumaïla Cissé
Minister of Finance and Commerce
Mali

David C. Cole (and co-author
  Betty F. Slade)
Consultants
Formerly of the Harvard Institute for
  International Development
United States

Zéphirin Diabré
Minister of Finance
Burkino Faso[1]

Note: The affiliations and titles are those at the time of the seminar.
[1]Zépherin Diabré was not present at the seminar but submitted a paper.

Patrick Downes
Assistant Director
Monetary and Exchange Affairs
* Department*
International Monetary Fund

Michael Foster
Head of the Africa Economics
* Department*
Overseas Development Administration
United Kingdom

Peter S. Heller
Senior Advisor
Fiscal Affairs Department
International Monetary Fund

Hiroyuki Hino
Assistant Director
African Department
International Monetary Fund

Ravi Kanbur
Chief Economist
Africa Region
World Bank

Basant Kapur
Professor in the Department of
* Economics and Statistics at the*
* National University of Singapore*
Singapore

Masako Ii
Associate Professor
Faculty of Economics
Yokohama National University
Japan

Jacob Mwanza
Governor
Bank of Zambia
Zambia

Tadahiko Nakagawa
Chief Representative in Paris
Export-Import Bank of Japan
Japan

John Nellis
Senior Manager
Private Sector Development
* Department*
World Bank

Dahlan M. Sutalaksana
Special Advisor to the Minister of
* Finance*
Indonesia

Tetsuji Tanaka
Senior Bank Supervisor with the Bank
* of Japan and Special Economic*
* Advisor to the President of the*
* Kyrgyz Republic and Kyrgyz*
* National Bank*
Japan

Peter Warutere
Group Managing Editor
Economic Review
Kenya

Yasuo Yokoyama
Senior Regional Coordinator
Mitsui & Co. Ltd.
South Africa
(Japan)

Shahid Yusuf
Lead Economist
Eastern Africa Region
World Bank

Participants

Chérif Daoussan Bichara
Chief of the Support Group in charge of
* managing adjustment-related projects*
Ministry of Planning and Cooperation
Chad

George Anthony Chigora
Deputy Secretary
Ministry of Finance
Zimbabwe

José Fondo
National Director
Ministry of Finance and Planning
Mozambique

Toshio Fujinuma
Chief Representative
The Overseas Economic Cooperation
*   Fund*
Japan

Shigeto Hashiyama
Representative in Paris
Export-Import Bank of Japan
Japan

Yoshio Hatakeyama
Deputy Chief Representative in Paris
Export-Import Bank of Japan
Japan

Hitoshi Hirata
Representative
The Overseas Economic Cooperation
*   Fund*
Japan

Ben Ibe
Deputy Director
Multilateral Institutions Department
Federal Ministry of Finance
Nigeria

Yasushi Kanzaki
First Secretary
Japanese Delegation to the OECD
Japan

Asahiko Karashima
Trainee
The Overseas Economic Cooperation
*   Fund*
Japan

Joseph Kinyua
Financial Secretary
Ministry of Finance
Kenya

Akihiko Koenuma
Representative
The Overseas Economic Cooperation
*   Fund*
Japan

Namala Koné
Director General of Public Debt
Mali

Tomoko Kurata
Special Assistant
The Overseas Economic Cooperation
*   Fund*
Japan

José Leandro
European Commission
Belgium

Edouard Luboya
Executive Secretary
National Association of Zaïrian
*   Enterprises*
Zaïre

Masato Matsui
Chief
Development Finance Division
Ministry of Finance
Japan

Said Youssou Mondoha
Secretary General of the Ministry of
*   Finance*
Comoros

Mary Muduuli
Commissioner for Economic Planning
Ministry of Planning and Economic
*   Development*
Uganda

Jean-Philippe Njeck
Advisor to the Minister of Economy
*   and Finance*
Ministry of Finance
Cameroon

Kunio Okamura
Director, 2nd Division
Operations Department III
The Overseas Economic Cooperation
Fund
Japan

Kakutoshi Oohori
Trainee
The Overseas Economic Cooperation
Fund
Japan

Luc Oyoubi
Director-General
Ministry of Finance, Economy, Budget,
and Participations
Gabon

Marinela Ribas
Executive Director
National Bank of Angola
Angola

Mitsuo Sakaba
Counselor
Japanese Delegation to the OECD
Japan

Aliou Seck
Secretary General
Ministry of Economy, Finance, and
Planning
Senegal

Robert Sharer
Division Chief
African Department
International Monetary Fund

Hitoshi Shimura
Deputy Director
Development Finance Division
Ministry of Finance
Japan

Kazuhiro Tohei
Representative in Paris
Export-Import Bank of Japan
Japan

Joseph Tsika
Chief of Staff of Ministry of
Finance, and Coordinator of
Technical Unit
Interministerial Committee for the
Coordination and the Monitoring of
Implementation of Structural
Adjustment Policies
Republic of the Congo

Yasufumi Uenishi
Special Officer for Research and
Planning
Development Institutions Division
Ministry of Finance
Japan

Yoshiko Urakawa
Co-financing Officer, Africa Region
Office of the Regional Vice-President
World Bank

Laura Wallace
Senior Public Affairs Officer
External Relations Department
International Monetary Fund

Takayuki Yahata
Development Finance Division
Ministry of Finance
Japan

Gebreselassie Yosief
Director of the Budget
Ministry of Finance
Eritrea